TO MY FIRST YEAR TEACHERS WITH LOVE

Bernard H. Jones, Jr

Copyright © 2024 by
Bernard H. Jones Jr

ALL RIGHTS RESERVED. NO part of this book may be reproduced or transmitted in any form by any means, electronic or mechanical, including photocopying and recording, or by any information storage and retrieval system, except as may be expressly permitted in writing from the author.

ISBN:
979-8-3306-9238-5 (Paperback)
979-8-3306-9239-2 (Ebook)

Testimonials

Bernie Jones initiated a program that teaches the latest teaching practices and skills new teachers need to know in order to be effective in the classroom. Teaching is an art. Effective teachers focus on student learning and accountability. This is a must read for novice educators all around the world.

Dr. Steven Kalson

Mr. Jones has always been welcoming, supportive, and dedicated to helping his colleagues and students succeed in the field of education. It is no surprise that he decided to write this book to help new educators build strength academically, emotionally, and strategically. Bernard you are to be commended!

Dr. Barren Harvey

I'm just blown away by everything you've poured into this book. Thank you for looking out for generation upon generations to come with regards to the essentials that will make students better prepared for what life has to offer. Thank you also for generously giving so much of your time, energy, and efforts into it.

Dr. Alvin Jones

Bernard's book is very well done. The minute I started the intensive review, I knew it was exactly what I was looking for. You are to be commended sir!

Father Thomas Smith

I am a first year teacher with overwhelming struggles with classroom management, class size, differentiation of instruction, pacing, and collaboration. Mr. Jones' techniques are not only helpful so far, but I can see the difference that it is already making in my class. Thank you for allowing me to get a sneak preview of your book at the signing. I will pass this on to other educators.

Sue Lampkin

TABLE OF CONTENTS

Introduction 1

Chapter 1 Building a Strong Foundation 6

Chapter 2 Mastering Classroom Management 24

Chapter 3 Lesson Planning for Success 37

Chapter 4 The Power of Relationships 51

Chapter 5 Adaptability and Growth 66

Chapter 6 Spiritual Foundations in Teaching 80

Chapter 7 Overcoming Challenges 97

Chapter 8 Emotional and Social Intelligence 107

Chapter 9 Tools for Continued Success 114

Chapter 10 Creating a Lasting Impact 124

Conclusion 139

INTRODUCTION

Teaching is more than just a profession; it is a calling that demands patience, dedication, and a deep-seated belief in the potential of every student. In today's rapidly changing educational landscape, teachers are not just imparting knowledge; they are shaping lives, molding futures, and laying the groundwork for a better society. However, the challenges that educators face today are more complex and multifaceted than ever before. This book is written to serve as a guiding light for teachers who are striving to overcome these challenges, build strong foundations in their classrooms, and create lasting, positive impacts on their students.

Purpose of the Book

The purpose of this book is to empower educators by providing them with practical strategies, insights, and tools that have been honed through years of experience. This is not just another guide on teaching techniques; it is a comprehensive resource that addresses the full spectrum of challenges teachers face, from classroom management to lesson planning, from professional development to personal well-being.

Through this book, you will learn how to:

1. Build Strong Foundations:

- Establish clear boundaries and maintain a healthy work-life balance.
- Develop strong professional relationships with colleagues to foster a collaborative environment.
- Cultivate a positive mindset that sees every student as capable and gifted.

2. Enhance Classroom Management:

- Implement effective discipline strategies that create a structured and respectful classroom environment.
- Tailor instruction to meet the diverse needs of students, including those with Individual Education Plans (IEPs).
- Adapt to the unique challenges posed by large class sizes and varying levels of student engagement.

3. Optimize Instructional Planning:

- Design lessons that cater to different learning styles, whether auditory, kinesthetic, or visual.
- Integrate technology into your teaching practices to enhance student learning and engagement.

- Use assessment methods that not only evaluate student progress but also inform future instruction.

4. Promote Personal and Professional Growth:

- Embrace continuous learning through reading, research, and collaboration with peers.
- Reflect on your teaching practices regularly to identify areas for improvement.
- Develop effective time management and organizational skills to handle the demands of the profession.

5. Foster a Positive Learning Environment:

- Build strong, meaningful relationships with your students both inside and outside the classroom.
- Create a sense of community within your classroom where every student feels valued and supported.
- Focus on the emotional and spiritual well-being of your students, encouraging empathy, resilience, and a love for learning.

Challenges Teachers Face Today

Today's educators are navigating a complex and often overwhelming array of challenges. These challenges include:

Differentiation of Instruction: With classrooms becoming increasingly diverse, teachers must customize their instruction to meet the individual needs of every student, including those with special educational needs. This requires a deep understanding of different learning styles and the ability to adapt lessons accordingly.

Technology Integration: While technology offers incredible opportunities for enhancing learning, it also presents challenges. Teachers must stay abreast of the latest technological trends, understand how to effectively integrate them into their lessons, and manage the potential distractions they may bring.

Classroom Discipline: Maintaining discipline in the classroom is more challenging than ever, with students coming from varied backgrounds and dealing with a range of social and emotional issues. Teachers must find ways to enforce rules consistently while remaining empathetic and supportive.

Time Management: The demands on teachers' time are immense, from planning and delivering lessons to grading assignments, communicating with parents, and participating in professional development. Effective time management is crucial to prevent burnout and maintain a high level of teaching quality.

School Safety: In a world where concerns about school safety are increasingly prevalent, teachers must be vigilant and prepared to handle a wide range of situations, from bullying to more severe threats.

Burnout and Mental Health: The emotional toll of teaching is significant, and without proper support and self-care, many teachers experience burnout. This book will provide strategies for managing stress, maintaining mental health, and finding joy in the teaching profession.

Communication and Collaboration: Effective communication with students, parents, and colleagues is essential but often challenging. Teachers must navigate these relationships with sensitivity and clarity to ensure that everyone is working toward the same goals.

This book is designed to be your companion in the journey of teaching. It will provide you with practical advice, real-life examples, and reflective exercises to help you overcome the obstacles you face and thrive in your role as an educator. Whether you are a new teacher looking to build a strong foundation or a seasoned educator seeking fresh insights, this book will guide you toward becoming the best teacher you can be.

By focusing on building relationships, cultivating a positive mindset, and staying true to your spiritual and emotional foundations, you will not only become a more effective teacher but also create a classroom environment where your students can thrive. Together, we will explore the art and science of teaching, and how you can make a lasting impact on the lives of your students.

Chapter 1
Building a Strong Foundation

In any endeavor, the strength of your foundation determines the stability and success of your efforts. This is especially true in the field of education, where the foundation you build as a teacher sets the stage for everything else that follows. From the way you manage your classroom to the relationships you build with your students, your ability to create a positive and effective learning environment begins with a solid foundation.

Building a strong foundation in teaching is not just about mastering the technical aspects of the job; it's about cultivating the right mindset, setting clear boundaries, and establishing core principles that will guide you throughout your career. This chapter is dedicated to helping you lay down that foundation, ensuring that you are well-equipped to handle the challenges and opportunities that come your way.

Why Building a Strong Foundation Matters

In the early years of teaching, it can be tempting to focus solely on the immediate tasks at hand—planning lessons, grading papers, and managing classroom behavior. However, without a strong foundation, these tasks can quickly become overwhelming, leading to burnout and frustration. A well-built foundation serves as a stabilizing force, allowing you to navigate the complexities of teaching with confidence and resilience.

A strong foundation also enables you to create a classroom environment where students feel safe, supported, and motivated to learn. It allows you to be consistent in your expectations and interactions, which in turn helps students develop trust and respect for you as their teacher. When students know what to expect, they are more likely to engage in the learning process and take ownership of their education.

Core Components of a Strong Foundation

Setting Boundaries: One of the most crucial elements of a strong foundation is the ability to set and maintain boundaries. This includes establishing a healthy work-life balance, defining your role as an educator, and ensuring that you have the time and energy to take care of yourself. Setting boundaries also involves being clear about your expectations for students, colleagues, and administrators, and consistently enforcing those expectations.

Cultivating a Positive Mindset: Your mindset as a teacher plays a significant role in your success. A positive, growth-oriented mindset allows you to see challenges as opportunities for learning and improvement. It also helps you maintain a sense of purpose and passion for teaching, even in the face of difficulties. By cultivating a mindset that views all students as capable and gifted, you create an environment where everyone has the opportunity to succeed.

Building Strong Relationships: Relationships are at the heart of effective teaching. Whether it's your relationships with students, colleagues, or parents, the connections you build can greatly impact the success of your teaching efforts. A strong foundation includes the ability to build and maintain positive, respectful relationships that foster collaboration, trust, and mutual support.

Establishing Core Values: Your core values as an educator serve as the guiding principles for your teaching practice. These values shape your decisions, influence your interactions with students, and inform your approach to challenges. By clearly defining your core values, you ensure that your actions are aligned with your beliefs and that you are consistently working towards your goals as a teacher.

Spiritual and Emotional Well-being: Teaching is a demanding profession that requires a strong sense of spiritual and emotional well-being. This aspect of your foundation involves finding ways to stay connected to your inner self, whether through prayer, meditation, or other practices that help you maintain a sense of balance and peace. By prioritizing your spiritual and emotional well-being, you can remain resilient in the face of challenges and continue to inspire and uplift your students.

The Influence of Spiritual Foundation on Teaching

Your spiritual foundation plays a crucial role in shaping your approach to teaching, providing you with the inner strength, resilience, and sense of purpose needed to steer the challenges of the profession. Let's explore how each aspect of this foundation influences your work as an educator.

A. Inner Peace and Calm

Teaching is a demanding job that can often lead to stress, frustration, and burnout. However, maintaining a strong spiritual foundation helps you cultivate inner peace and calm, allowing you to approach each day with a clear mind and steady heart. This inner peace acts as a stabilizing force, allowing you to remain composed even in difficult situations. Whether it's handling disruptive behavior in the classroom or managing the pressures of administrative tasks, a calm demeanor allows you to think more clearly, make better decisions, and create a positive learning environment for your students.

Inner peace also influences how you interact with your students. When you are calm, you are better able to listen, empathize, and respond thoughtfully to their needs. This helps build trust and rapport, making students feel more comfortable and supported in your classroom. Moreover, your calm presence can have a soothing effect on your students, helping to create an atmosphere conducive to learning and personal growth.

B. Belief in a Higher Power

A belief in a higher power through faith serves as a guiding principle in your teaching journey. This faith gives you the strength to persevere, even when faced with challenges that seem insurmountable. By trusting that there is a greater purpose behind your work, you are able to approach each day with a sense of mission and dedication.

Faith, combined with action, becomes a powerful tool for success. It encourages you to put in the necessary effort, knowing that your work is not in vain. This belief can also inspire your students, as they see you leading by example, working diligently, and remaining committed to their growth and development. Through faith, you convey the message that success is achievable through hard work, perseverance, and trust in something greater than ourselves.

C. Keep Moving Forward

Teaching can be filled with setbacks and disappointments, whether it's a lesson that didn't go as planned, a difficult student, or challenges outside of the classroom. However, a strong spiritual foundation instills in you the resilience to keep moving forward, no matter the obstacles. This resilience is rooted in the belief that every challenge is an opportunity for growth and that perseverance will ultimately lead to success.

By embodying this principle, you model for your students the importance of persistence and determination. You teach them that failure is not the end, but rather a stepping stone toward improvement. This mindset not only helps you overcome difficulties but also inspires your students to adopt a similar attitude, fostering a classroom culture of perseverance and continuous learning.

D. The Power of Prayer

Prayer is a powerful tool in your spiritual arsenal, providing you with guidance, strength, and a sense of connection to something greater than yourself. In the context of teaching, prayer can serve as a source of comfort and clarity, helping you to navigate the complexities of your role with wisdom and grace. Whether it's praying for patience, understanding, or the well-being of your students, this practice reinforces your commitment to your work and reminds you of the higher purpose behind it.

Believing in the power of prayer also instills a sense of trust and surrender. It encourages you to do your best and leave the rest in the hands of a higher power, reducing the burden of trying to control every outcome. This trust allows you to approach your work with confidence, knowing that you are supported and guided in your efforts.

E. Serve with Heartfelt Intention

Service is at the core of teaching, and when it comes from the heart, it is not only rewarding but also transformative. Your spiritual foundation teaches you that genuine service—motivated by love, compassion, and a desire to make a positive impact—will be rewarded in ways that go beyond material recognition. This belief drives you to give your best to your students, not for accolades, but because you truly care about their success and well-being.

Serving with heartfelt intention also helps you connect more deeply with your students. When they sense that your actions are motivated by genuine concern for their growth, they are more likely to respond positively and engage fully in the learning process. This approach fosters a nurturing and supportive classroom environment where students feel valued and empowered to reach their full potential.

In essence, your spiritual foundation is the bedrock of your teaching practice. It provides you with the peace, faith, resilience, and sense of purpose needed to be an effective and compassionate educator. By integrating these spiritual principles into your daily work, you not only enhance your own well-being but also create a positive and impactful learning experience for your students.

To maintain a strong spiritual foundation in your daily routine as an educator, you can incorporate specific practices and beliefs that not only nurture your own well-being but also positively impact those around you. Here's how you can integrate these principles into your day-to-day life:

Spend Time Being Interested in the Needs of Your Colleagues and Students

Taking a genuine interest in the lives of your colleagues and students goes beyond the professional realm and fosters deeper connections. By spending time understanding their needs, aspirations, and challenges, you create a supportive and empathetic environment. This might involve checking in with a colleague who seems stressed, listening to a student's concerns, or simply engaging in small talk to show that you care.

Look for the Best in Others—Students and Colleagues

One of the most powerful practices you can adopt is looking for the best in others. This involves consciously focusing on the strengths, talents, and positive qualities of your students and colleagues, rather than dwelling on their shortcomings. By recognizing and affirming the good in others, you help to uplift and encourage them, which can lead to increased confidence, motivation, and a more positive atmosphere in the classroom and workplace.

Service Before Self Attitude

Adopting a service-before-self attitude means prioritizing the needs of others before your own, which is a key aspect of a spiritually grounded approach to teaching. This doesn't mean neglecting your own well-being, but rather approaching your work with a mindset of selflessness and dedication. It's about being willing to go the extra mile for your students and colleagues, whether that's staying after school to help a struggling student, volunteering for a school event, or supporting a colleague in need.

Mindset & Attitude

As an educator, cultivating a mindset that views all students as capable and gifted is essential for creating an inclusive and empowering learning environment. This perspective not only shapes how you approach teaching but also has a profound impact on how your students see themselves and their abilities. Here's how you can develop and maintain this mindset:

A. Recognize that All Students Are Unique and Creative

Every student brings their own unique set of strengths, talents, and perspectives to the classroom. By acknowledging and celebrating this diversity, you create a space where each student feels valued and understood. This involves seeing beyond traditional measures of success and recognizing the different ways students express their creativity and problem-solving abilities. Whether a student excels in artistic endeavors, shows strong interpersonal skills, or demonstrates an aptitude for logical thinking, it's important to affirm their unique contributions. This recognition encourages students to take pride in their individuality and motivates them to engage more fully in their learning journey.

B. Understand That All Students Are Capable of Learning

A key component of this mindset is the belief that all students are capable of learning, regardless of their starting point or learning style. While students may differ in how they absorb and process information, the ultimate goal remains the same: to help them achieve the learning objectives set before them. By offering varied learning experiences tailored to different needs—whether through visual aids, hands-on activities, or interactive discussions—you ensure that every student has the opportunity to grasp the concepts being taught. This approach respects each student's learning process and fosters an environment where diverse learning paths are not just accommodated but celebrated.

C. Use Evidence-Based Strategies to Support Learning

Implementing evidence-based strategies is essential for supporting student learning effectively. These strategies, grounded in research, provide proven methods for enhancing student engagement, understanding, and retention of material. Whether it's using formative assessments to gauge understanding, incorporating cooperative learning techniques, or applying scaffolding to support complex tasks, these practices ensure that you are using the most effective tools available to help your students succeed. By relying on evidence-based strategies, you demonstrate a commitment to using the best possible methods to support all students in reaching their full potential.

Techniques to Maintain a Positive Attitude

A. Look at the Situation with an Optimistic Approach, Not Pessimistic

When faced with challenges, it's important to focus on the potential solutions rather than dwelling on the problems. By adopting an optimistic outlook, you can see obstacles as opportunities for growth and improvement. This shift in perspective helps to maintain a positive attitude, making it easier to navigate difficulties with resilience and determination.

B. Practice Gratitude

Regularly practicing gratitude helps you stay grounded and appreciative of the positives in your life, even during tough times. Taking a moment to reflect on what you're thankful for—whether it's supportive colleagues, a successful lesson, or simply the opportunity to make a difference—can uplift your spirits and reinforce a positive mindset.

C. Set Goals That Are Attainable and Realistic

Setting attainable and realistic goals provides a sense of direction and accomplishment. When your goals are manageable, you can achieve them more easily, which boosts your confidence and keeps you motivated. This approach prevents you from feeling overwhelmed and helps you stay focused on what's achievable.

Reflection & Growth

Regularly Reflecting on Teaching Practices

To ensure that you are continually building on your foundation as an educator, regular reflection on your teaching practices is crucial. This process involves several key components:

Consider Goals: Regularly revisiting your educational goals helps you stay focused on your objectives and assess whether your current practices align with them. It's important to set clear, achievable goals and measure your progress toward meeting them.

Student Observations with Anecdotal Notes: Observing students and taking anecdotal notes allows you to track their progress and identify areas for improvement. These observations provide valuable insights into how students are responding to different teaching strategies and can inform adjustments to your approach.

Review Individualized Education Programs (IEPs): Checking IEPs ensures that the specific needs of students are being met both in and out of the classroom. This review helps you make necessary adjustments to support each student's unique learning requirements effectively.

Sharpening Teaching Strategies: Continuously refining your teaching strategies based on reflections and feedback helps you stay effective and responsive to students' needs. This might involve experimenting with new techniques or adapting existing ones to enhance learning outcomes.

Modeling Expectations and Lessons with Follow-Up: Demonstrating clear expectations and following up on lessons reinforces learning and helps students understand what is required of them. This practice supports consistent and effective teaching.

Continuous Collaboration with Educators and Students: Engaging in ongoing collaboration with fellow educators and students fosters a supportive learning environment. Sharing experiences, strategies, and feedback can lead to improved practices and mutual growth.

Taking Good Notes (Journal): Keeping a journal of your teaching experiences, reflections, and observations provides a record of what works well and what could be improved. This ongoing documentation helps you track your development and make informed decisions about your teaching practice.

Key Lessons from Early in Your Career

Several key lessons learned early in your career continue to guide you today:

Flexibility in Lesson Planning: A well-prepared lesson is important, but flexibility is essential to address the dynamic needs of the classroom. Sometimes, stepping away from a rigid lesson plan to respond to immediate classroom needs can be more effective in supporting student learning.

Support for Different Learning Styles: Understanding that a lesson must be adaptable to accommodate various learning styles is crucial. Flexibility allows you to tailor your approach to meet the diverse needs of students, ensuring that everyone has the opportunity to succeed.

The Learning Journey: Recognizing that learning is not just about arriving at the correct answer but also about the process of discovery is fundamental. Emphasizing the journey toward understanding encourages deeper engagement and helps students appreciate the value of learning beyond immediate results.

By integrating these reflective practices and lessons into your daily routine, you can continue to grow as an educator and provide a more effective and responsive learning experience for your students.

ANECDOTE

CAN'T TEACH A FISH TO CLIMB A TREE

Imagine trying to teach a fish to climb a tree. It sounds absurd, right? This anecdote serves as a powerful metaphor for understanding the importance of recognizing and leveraging individuals' natural strengths and talents in education. Here's how this story reflects a thoughtful and effective approach to teaching:

Understanding Natural Strengths and Talents

The essence of the "Can't teach a fish to climb a tree" story is that every individual has unique strengths and talents. Just as a fish is perfectly adapted to swim rather than climb, students have their own inherent abilities that might not align with traditional educational methods. Forcing a student to excel in areas where they lack natural aptitude can lead to frustration and minimal success. Instead, recognizing and nurturing each student's strengths allows them to thrive and achieve their best.

The Importance of a Support System

Just as a fish needs water to thrive, students need the proper support system to succeed. This support system includes a variety of tools and resources that cater to diverse learning needs. In the classroom, this might involve providing books, technology, manipulatives, number lines, and graphic organizers. Each of these resources helps create a learning environment that accommodates different learning styles and needs. For teachers, support might include professional development, collaborative planning, and access to educational materials that enhance their teaching effectiveness.

Tailoring Education to Individual Needs

The story highlights that education should not be a one-size-fits-all approach. Instead, it should be flexible and responsive to the diverse needs of students. By understanding that students have different strengths and learning styles, educators can tailor their instruction to provide meaningful and engaging learning experiences. This approach not only helps students feel more confident and capable but also improves their overall academic success.

Creating an Inclusive Learning Environment

The story also underscores the importance of creating an inclusive learning environment where every student feels valued and supported. Just as it would be unreasonable to expect a fish to climb a tree, it is unrealistic to expect all students to excel in the same way. By embracing this diversity and providing the necessary tools and accommodations, educators can help all students reach their full potential.

Chapter 2

Mastering Classroom Management

Classroom management is one of the most essential elements of a successful learning environment. Without structure and control, even the most well-planned lessons can fall apart. As a teacher, your ability to maintain order, set clear expectations, and foster a positive atmosphere directly impacts the effectiveness of your instruction and the success of your students. But classroom management isn't just about rules and discipline; it's about creating an environment where students feel safe, respected, and motivated to learn.

In this chapter, we will explore strategies to help you maintain control in your classroom while fostering a positive learning environment. The key to this balance is consistency—students need to know what to expect, both in terms of behavior and learning expectations. A well-managed classroom provides a sense of structure, which is vital for students to thrive academically and socially. This begins with setting clear rules and expectations and applying them consistently, so that students know exactly what is required of them.

However, managing a classroom goes beyond enforcing rules. It requires understanding the diverse needs of your students, including their different learning styles. Some students may need more visual aids, others may benefit from hands-on activities, while some respond better to auditory instruction. By engaging students through a variety of teaching methods, you create an inclusive environment where each student can succeed.

Discipline is another essential component, but it must be handled with both empathy and firmness. While some behavior requires immediate correction, it's equally important to understand the reasons behind certain actions. Building strong relationships with your students allows you to address discipline in a way that respects their individuality, while still maintaining authority and structure in the classroom.

As we move through this chapter, we'll also explore the challenges of managing diverse classroom dynamics. Each classroom is a unique blend of personalities, backgrounds, and abilities, and effective management requires adapting your strategies to meet these varied needs. One size does not fit all, which is why the anecdote "Can't fix a washing machine with refrigerator parts" is so relevant. You can't apply the same solution to every problem or expect a uniform approach to work for every student.

Instead, you must customize your management techniques to fit the unique dynamics of your classroom.

By the end of this chapter, you'll have a solid toolkit of classroom management strategies that you can apply in your own teaching practice. From maintaining consistency and engaging students through various learning styles, to addressing discipline with empathy and managing a diverse classroom, the goal is to create a learning environment where both you and your students can succeed. This chapter will also conclude with a practical checklist and an action plan that you can implement immediately to strengthen your classroom management skills.

Mastering classroom management isn't about perfection, but progress. Each day presents new challenges and opportunities to grow as an educator. With the right strategies in place, you'll create a positive, structured environment where learning can flourish.

Tips on Ensuring Consistency:

A. Consistent schedule—model changes

Having a consistent daily schedule helps create predictability, which is essential for students to feel secure and know what to expect. When changes to the schedule are necessary, it's important to model these adjustments for students. Demonstrating flexibility while maintaining structure reassures students that even when things don't go as planned, the class will still operate smoothly. This fosters a stable environment where students can focus on learning rather than worrying about disruptions.

B. Clearly defined expectations with examples, justification, and scenarios

Setting clear expectations from the outset is crucial for classroom management. By providing examples, explaining the reasons behind the rules, and using real-life scenarios, students can understand not only what is expected but also why those rules are in place. This promotes a sense of fairness and transparency, allowing students to internalize the rules rather than just follow them blindly. It also gives them the context they need to apply these expectations in various situations.

C. Sequence modeled and revisited

It's important to continually model the sequence of expected behaviors and routines. Repeatedly revisiting these sequences, especially early in the school year, helps reinforce the behaviors you want to see. Regular reminders and practice ensure that expectations become second nature to students. Over time, these routines contribute to a well-managed classroom where students know exactly what is required of them without constant instruction.

D. Whatever you say, do

Consistency between what you say and what you do is key to building trust and respect in the classroom. If students observe that you follow through on your words, whether it's enforcing a rule or rewarding positive behavior, they are more likely to take your expectations seriously. Inconsistent follow-through can lead to confusion and erode your authority, making classroom management more challenging.

E. Teacher and colleagues on the same page

It's important that teachers and any supporting staff members maintain a united front when it comes to classroom rules and expectations. Consistency across all adults in the classroom ensures that students receive the same message, no matter who is present. When teachers and colleagues enforce the same rules in the same manner, students understand that these expectations are non-negotiable, creating a cohesive and well-regulated environment.

Strategies to Engage Students:

A. Differentiated instruction—one size doesn't fit all

Differentiated instruction recognizes that students have diverse needs, strengths, and ways of learning. This approach involves tailoring lessons to meet those differences, ensuring that each student can access the material in a way that suits them best. By using varied instructional methods, you can support visual, auditory, and kinesthetic learners, allowing each student to succeed on their own terms. Understanding that one approach doesn't work for everyone is the foundation for effective teaching.

B. Different teaching methods—auditory, hands-on, kinesthetic

Incorporating various teaching methods is key to reaching all learners. Some students thrive on auditory learning, while others need to engage physically through hands-on or kinesthetic activities. By providing a variety of ways to learn the same material, you allow students to grasp concepts in a manner that aligns with their preferred style. Whether through listening, movement, or hands-on manipulation, these varied approaches ensure that learning is accessible to all.

C. Whole group, conferences, individualized instruction

Using a mix of whole group instruction, one-on-one conferences, and individualized learning plans helps address different student needs. Whole group instruction introduces the lesson and builds a common foundation, while conferences and individualized attention allow for personalized support. These methods ensure that no student is left behind and that each gets the specific guidance needed to succeed.

D. Multimodal approach

A multimodal approach combines visual, auditory, and kinesthetic elements into lessons. By delivering content in multiple ways, you ensure that students can interact with the material in the way that best suits their learning preferences. For instance, a lesson might include visual aids, hands-on activities, and a verbal explanation, allowing all students to process the information in their preferred way.

E. Give students options—give them ownership and flexibility

Offering students choices in how they engage with the material encourages ownership of their learning. When students can choose between different methods—such as writing, creating a visual project, or participating in a discussion—they feel more empowered and invested in their success. Flexibility allows them to take control of their education and fosters a sense of responsibility.

F. Positive, optimistic attitude

Maintaining a positive and optimistic attitude is essential for creating a supportive learning environment. Students are more likely to engage with the material when they feel encouraged and believe in their ability to succeed. A positive atmosphere boosts motivation and helps students overcome challenges, fostering a classroom culture where learning thrives.

Managing Diverse Classroom Dynamics:

A. Cultural sensitivity

Understanding and respecting the diverse cultural backgrounds of your students is essential for creating an inclusive environment. Cultural sensitivity means being aware of and appreciating differences in language, traditions, and customs, while making sure that no student feels marginalized or misunderstood. This includes incorporating culturally relevant materials, acknowledging different perspectives, and avoiding biases that could negatively affect students. By fostering an atmosphere of acceptance, you ensure all students feel valued.

B. Flexibility—can't be too rigid

Classrooms are dynamic environments, and a rigid approach can stifle both learning and relationships. Flexibility in teaching methods, classroom management, and communication allows you to adapt to the needs of your students. Whether it's adjusting lesson plans, offering alternative assessments, or allowing students to express themselves in different ways, being adaptable helps you meet the diverse needs of your classroom. Flexibility shows students that you are responsive to their unique situations and willing to work with them.

C. Model good behavior to colleagues and students

Teachers set the tone for classroom behavior. By consistently modeling respect, empathy, and patience, you demonstrate how students should treat one another. Good behavior includes active listening, addressing conflicts calmly, and showing respect for all opinions. When you model these behaviors, both students and colleagues are more likely to mirror them, creating a more positive and respectful classroom atmosphere.

D. Good communication

Effective communication is key to managing classroom dynamics. Clear, open, and respectful communication ensures that students understand your expectations and feel comfortable expressing their thoughts and concerns. This also involves listening actively and empathetically to students, validating their experiences, and encouraging dialogue. Good communication fosters trust and helps resolve conflicts before they escalate, ensuring a respectful and inclusive environment.

E. Consistency

Consistency in rules, expectations, and behavior management is crucial for creating a stable and respectful classroom environment. When students know what to expect, they feel more secure and are more likely to engage positively. Consistency also ensures that all students are treated fairly, regardless of their backgrounds or abilities, which is important for building trust and maintaining respect. A consistent approach helps students understand that you are reliable and committed to their well-being.

Addressing Discipline Issues:

A. Obtainable expectations

Setting clear, obtainable expectations from the outset ensures that students understand what is required of them. When expectations are realistic and achievable, students are more likely to meet them, reducing the need for disciplinary measures. It's important to explain the reasons behind rules so students understand that they exist for their growth and safety, not as arbitrary constraints. Setting achievable goals allows students to take responsibility for their behavior while providing a framework for accountability.

B. Compassionate and good listener

Addressing discipline issues with empathy requires active listening and understanding the root cause of a student's behavior. Sometimes, misbehavior stems from underlying issues, such as personal challenges or frustration with the material. By showing compassion and listening to their side of the story, you can address the problem more effectively and create a supportive environment.

Students are more likely to respond positively to discipline when they feel heard and understood.

C. Treat others like you want to be treated—treat like a human

This principle of empathy emphasizes the importance of treating students with dignity and respect, even during disciplinary situations. When students are treated fairly and with kindness, they are more likely to respond positively and take responsibility for their actions. Approaching discipline with humanity means acknowledging that students make mistakes and need guidance rather than punishment, reinforcing the idea that you're there to help them grow.

D. Be firm but fair—treat all the same, no favorites

Firmness in discipline is essential for maintaining control and respect in the classroom. However, being firm doesn't mean being harsh or unfair. Balancing firmness with fairness ensures that students understand the consequences of their actions, while also feeling that they are treated equally. Consistency in enforcing rules, without showing favoritism, builds trust and ensures that students know what to expect, creating an environment where discipline is seen as just and reasonable.

E. Constantly review and model—include teachers and students

Discipline is not a one-time action but an ongoing process. Continuously reviewing and modeling appropriate behavior with both students and colleagues helps reinforce expectations. When students see positive behavior consistently modeled by teachers, it becomes easier for them to follow suit. Including other teachers in the process ensures that discipline approaches are consistent throughout the school, reinforcing a collective standard of behavior. Modeling empathy and fairness shows students that discipline can be both compassionate and firm.

ANECDOTE

CAN'T FIX A WASHING MACHINE WITH REFRIGERATOR PARTS

I often use cars as an analogy: you can't fix a Rolls Royce with Buick parts. While some parts may be interchangeable, most are specialized to fit the specific make and model. The same is true for instruction—teaching strategies can't be one-size-fits-all. Just like different cars need different parts, students have unique learning needs that require tailored approaches. For example, if a student struggles with math, I might introduce more visual aids, like graphic organizers, or provide hands-on tools like number lines and manipulatives. For students with disabilities, specialized equipment, technology, or even specific seating arrangements can make a world of difference. By custom-tailoring instruction to fit each student, you're addressing their individual needs, just like using the right parts to fix the right car, leading to fewer challenges and better results in the classroom.

Chapter 3

Lesson Planning for Success

Effective lesson planning is the cornerstone of successful teaching. In this chapter, we will explore how to design lesson plans that not only meet educational standards but also cater to the diverse needs of all learners in your classroom. The ability to create engaging, adaptable, and student-centered lessons is crucial for fostering an inclusive and productive learning environment.

We will begin by discussing how to customize lessons to address the varying learning styles of auditory, kinesthetic, and visual learners. Recognizing that each student absorbs and processes information differently is key to crafting lessons that resonate with everyone. Next, we will delve into the integration of technology and inquiry-based learning methods. These modern tools and approaches can significantly enhance student engagement and deepen their understanding of the material.

Creating engaging, student-centered lessons involves more than just delivering content; it requires designing activities and assessments that motivate students and encourage active participation. We will cover strategies for making lessons more interactive and relevant to students' interests and needs.

Additionally, we will emphasize the importance of reflective practices and daily planning. Reflecting on each lesson helps you identify what worked well and what needs improvement, allowing you to continuously refine your teaching methods. Daily planning ensures that you are prepared and organized, maximizing the effectiveness of your instruction.

To support your journey, this chapter includes practical tools such as sample lesson plans and graphic organizers. These resources will help you implement the strategies discussed and develop personalized lesson plans that cater to the unique needs of your students.

By the end of this chapter, you will have a comprehensive understanding of how to create dynamic and effective lesson plans that not only meet educational goals but also support the diverse learning needs of your students.

Customizing Lesson Plans:

A. Assess students emotionally and academically

Before customizing your lesson plans, it's essential to understand each student's emotional and academic needs. Conducting assessments helps you gauge their current level of understanding, strengths, and areas for improvement. Emotional assessments can reveal students' engagement levels and comfort with the material, while academic assessments provide insights into their learning preferences and challenges. This understanding forms the foundation for tailoring your lessons effectively.

B. Read previous case files (Individualized Education Programs) to see what needs the student has and goals to meet those needs

Reviewing each student's Individualized Education Program (IEP) or any previous case files is crucial for understanding their specific needs and learning goals. These documents provide detailed information on the student's accommodations, modifications, and support required. Collaborate with colleagues or special education staff to adjust your approach based on these insights, ensuring that your lesson plans are aligned with the student's needs and objectives.

C. Same objectives/different learning experiences to meet those objectives

While the learning objectives should remain consistent, the methods for achieving them can vary to cater to different learning styles. For example, you might present the same content through various means: a lecture for auditory learners, hands-on activities for kinesthetic learners, and visual aids for visual learners. This approach ensures that all students can access the material in a way that suits their preferred learning style, promoting a deeper understanding of the content.

D. Auditory learners—verbal direction, group discussion, read-aloud, small group discussions, etc.

For auditory learners, incorporate techniques that emphasize listening and verbal processing. Use clear verbal instructions, engage students in group discussions, and conduct read-alouds to reinforce content. Small group discussions and verbal feedback also help auditory learners process information effectively through hearing and speaking.

E. Kinesthetic learners—movement, games, manipulatives, walk-around activities

Kinesthetic learners benefit from hands-on activities and movement. Include physical activities such as games, manipulatives, and interactive tasks in your lessons. Allow students to move around, use their hands to explore concepts, and engage in activities that involve physical interaction with the material, helping them absorb information through action and movement.

F. Visual learners—charts on wall, graphs, comparison pictures, examples posted, whiteboard, flash cards, PowerPoints, Google Doc assignments

Visual learners thrive on visual stimuli and organized information. Incorporate charts, graphs, comparison pictures, and other visual aids into your lessons. Use whiteboards for real-time demonstration, flash cards for quick reference, and multimedia tools like PowerPoints and Google Docs for visually rich content. These tools help visual learners connect with the material through sight and spatial organization.

Strategies to Employ Technology in Lesson Plans:

A. Student actively participates

To integrate technology effectively, ensure that it actively involves students in the learning process. Use interactive tools and platforms that require student engagement, such as online quizzes, collaborative projects, or virtual discussions. When students are actively participating with technology, they are more likely to stay focused and benefit from its use. This participation also helps maintain their interest and promotes a deeper understanding of the material.

B. Well-planned instruction with technology and backup in case technology isn't available

Plan your lessons with technology as a key component but also have a backup plan in case technical issues arise. Ensure that technology enhances your teaching by seamlessly integrating it into your instructional plan. For instance, prepare alternative activities or printouts that can be used if the technology fails. This preparation helps maintain the flow of the lesson and ensures that learning objectives are met even when technology isn't functioning as expected.

C. Variety of technology options

Utilize a range of technological tools and platforms to address different learning styles and preferences. Incorporate various types of technology, such as educational apps, interactive whiteboards, and multimedia presentations, to keep lessons dynamic and engaging. Offering multiple technology options can also help you address individual student needs and preferences, making learning more effective and personalized.

D. Supplement to instruction

Technology should act as a supplement to, not a replacement for, traditional teaching methods. Use it to enhance and reinforce the material you are teaching rather than as the sole focus of the lesson.

For example, use educational videos to illustrate complex concepts or interactive simulations to provide hands-on experiences. By integrating technology in a supportive role, you ensure that it complements your instruction and adds value to the learning experience.

E. Online resources as teaching aids

Incorporate online resources such as educational websites, digital libraries, and interactive learning tools as part of your lesson plans. These resources can provide additional information, support varied learning activities, and offer interactive elements that engage students. Make sure to select credible and relevant online resources that align with your lesson objectives and enhance the learning experience. By using online resources effectively, you can provide students with a richer and more diverse learning environment.

Incorporating Inquiry-Based Learning:

A. Teachers plan questions that guide students through activities

Incorporate inquiry-based learning by designing questions that guide students through their activities and investigations. Craft open-ended questions that encourage students to explore, analyze, and reflect on the topic. This approach helps students develop critical thinking skills and fosters a deeper understanding of the material. By guiding their learning through well-planned questions, you stimulate curiosity and encourage active participation, making the learning process more engaging and meaningful.

B. KWL chart (What I Know, What I Want to Know, What I Learned)

Utilize KWL charts to structure inquiry-based learning. Start by having students fill out the "What I Know" section to activate prior knowledge. Then, have them list what they want to learn in the "What I Want to Know" section, which directs their inquiry. Finally, after the lesson or unit, have students complete the "What I Learned" section to reflect on their new knowledge. This method helps students organize their thoughts, set learning goals, and review what they have discovered, reinforcing their learning and engagement.

C. Research groups

Incorporate research groups into your lessons to facilitate inquiry-based learning. Assign students to small groups and give them a specific question or topic to research. This collaborative approach allows students to delve into the subject matter, explore various sources, and synthesize information. Working in groups promotes teamwork and communication skills while allowing students to take ownership of their learning. Research groups also provide opportunities for peer learning and diverse perspectives, enhancing the overall learning experience.

D. Project with critical thinking questions

Integrate projects that include critical thinking questions to drive inquiry-based learning. Design projects that require students to apply their knowledge, analyze information, and solve problems. Encourage students to formulate their own questions and hypotheses, and guide them through the process of finding answers. This approach not only engages students but also helps them develop problem-solving and analytical skills. Critical thinking projects challenge students to think deeply and creatively, leading to a more profound understanding of the subject matter.

E. Presentations focused on getting other students to ask questions and think

Incorporate student presentations as a way to foster inquiry-based learning. Have students present their findings, ideas, or projects to the class, and encourage their peers to ask questions and provide feedback. This interactive element promotes a dynamic learning environment where students are both learners and teachers. Presentations that prompt questions and discussions help students articulate their understanding, engage with different viewpoints, and refine their ideas. This process enhances critical thinking and helps solidify their learning through peer interaction and reflection.

Adapting a Lesson Plan Based on Student Feedback or Performance

A. Using Data to Drive Instruction

To ensure that lesson plans are effective and meet the diverse needs of students, it's essential to adapt them based on various forms of feedback and performance data. This approach ensures that instruction is tailored to the actual needs and learning styles of students, rather than relying solely on a one-size-fits-all approach. Here's how you can use different types of data to refine and improve your lesson plans:

B. Anecdotal Notes

Anecdotal notes are informal records of observations about students' performance, behavior, and reactions during lessons. These notes provide qualitative insights into how students are engaging with the material. For example, if you notice that several students are struggling with a particular concept, you might adapt your lesson to include additional explanations, examples, or hands-on activities. By keeping detailed notes on each student's progress and challenges, you can make timely adjustments to support their learning needs.

C. Assessments

Formative and summative assessments offer valuable feedback on how well students have understood the lesson content. For instance, if a formative assessment (like a quick quiz or exit ticket) shows that students are not grasping a key concept, you can modify your lesson plan to revisit that concept. Adjustments might include providing additional practice opportunities, re-explaining the material using different methods, or incorporating more interactive elements to reinforce understanding.

D. Standardized Test Scores

Standardized test scores can help identify broader trends and areas where students may need additional support. If test scores reveal that students are consistently underperforming in specific areas, such as problem-solving or reading comprehension, you can adapt your lesson plans to focus more intensively on those areas. For instance, if students struggle with reading comprehension, you might incorporate more reading strategies and comprehension exercises into your lessons.

E. Community Survey Data

Surveys conducted within the school community can provide insights into students' interests, learning preferences, and any external factors affecting their education. If survey data indicates that students are particularly interested in a specific topic or have particular learning preferences, you can adjust your lesson plans to include elements that align with those interests or preferences. For example, if students show a preference for hands-on learning, you might integrate more experiential activities into your lessons.

F. Assignments and Chapter Tests

Performance on assignments and chapter tests can reveal how well students are mastering the material. If assignments show that students are consistently making mistakes or missing critical concepts, you might need to revisit those topics in your lesson plans. Additionally, if students excel in certain areas, you can provide more advanced or enrichment activities to challenge them further.

G. Behavior Records

Behavior records can provide insights into how students are responding to the lesson environment and instruction. If you notice patterns of disruptive behavior or disengagement, it might indicate that the lesson plan needs adjustment. For example, if students are frequently off-task during certain types of activities, you might need to modify the lesson to include more engaging or interactive elements.

H. Student Preferences

Taking into account students' preferences can significantly enhance engagement and learning outcomes. If you gather information about how students prefer to learn (e.g., through visual aids, hands-on activities, or group discussions), you can adapt your lesson plans to incorporate these preferences. Offering choices within assignments or activities can also increase student motivation and ownership of their learning.

I. Visual Representations of Data

Using visual tools such as line graphs, bar graphs, and stem-and-leaf plots can help you track and analyze student performance trends. For example, if a bar graph shows a decline in performance in a specific area, you can use this information to target that area with additional instruction or practice. Visual representations make it easier to identify patterns and make data-driven decisions to adjust your teaching strategies.

As we wrap up this chapter on lesson planning, it's clear that effective lesson planning is more than just outlining what will be taught; it's about creating a dynamic and adaptable framework that meets the diverse needs of your students. By customizing lessons to cater to auditory, kinesthetic, and visual learners, integrating technology and inquiry-based learning, and being responsive to feedback and performance data, you are laying the groundwork for a rich and engaging educational experience.

Remember, the essence of successful lesson planning lies in its flexibility and responsiveness. A well-crafted lesson plan is a living document that evolves based on the needs of your students. As you continue to refine your planning practices, keep in mind the importance of reflecting on your strategies, embracing a variety of teaching methods, and remaining open to adjustments.

The tools and techniques discussed in this chapter, such as using graphic organizers and incorporating technology, are designed to enhance your ability to connect with students and foster a more inclusive and effective learning environment. Take the time to experiment with these strategies, observe their impact, and adjust your approach as needed.

In the end, the goal is to create a classroom where every student feels valued and supported, where learning is personalized and engaging, and where you, as an educator, feel empowered to make a meaningful impact. By continually reflecting on and improving your lesson planning practices, you are setting the stage for student success and growth. Embrace the journey of teaching with enthusiasm and a commitment to excellence, and let your lesson plans reflect the best of what you have to offer.

Chapter 4

The Power of Relationships

In education, the foundation for effective teaching is built on relationships. The connections teachers form with their students, colleagues, and the wider community play a crucial role in shaping the classroom environment and influencing learning outcomes. *The Power of Relationships* explores how these relationships are essential for fostering a positive, collaborative, and growth-oriented space for both students and educators.

Developing strong relationships within the classroom goes beyond instructional methods; it taps into understanding students' unique needs, motivations, and aspirations. Teachers who take the time to connect with their students personally often find that they can break through academic barriers, as students who feel seen and valued are more motivated and engaged in their learning. This chapter delves into strategies for nurturing these connections, from simply showing genuine interest in students' lives to employing targeted techniques for engaging students emotionally and intellectually. The impact of a healthy teacher-student relationship extends far beyond academics—it shapes the entire educational experience and contributes significantly to a student's emotional and social development.

Equally important are the relationships teachers cultivate with their colleagues. Collaboration among educators is a key driver of professional growth, where exchanging ideas, resources, and feedback can lead to new insights and approaches to teaching. Fostering a supportive, collegial environment can also alleviate the pressures of the classroom, offering a space for shared problem-solving and continuous learning. This chapter explores how strong collegial relationships can elevate teaching practices, encourage professional growth, and build a more cohesive and effective learning community.

The role of community involvement is another essential aspect discussed here. Teachers do not operate in isolation; their work is often enriched by meaningful participation in the community. Whether through parent-teacher partnerships, volunteer work, or outreach initiatives, engaging with the community enhances the educational experience by creating opportunities for students to learn and grow outside the traditional classroom setting. When teachers actively involve themselves in community efforts, they help bridge the gap between school and the world beyond, fostering a holistic approach to education.

At the heart of this chapter is the idea that relationships take time and intentionality to grow. One simple but effective approach is the idea of "spending 10 minutes with each student a week in out-of-school conversations." These short but meaningful interactions can build rapport, demonstrate care, and create bonds that strengthen over time.

In this chapter, we'll explore various strategies for fostering meaningful connections both inside and outside the classroom, examine how teacher-student relationships directly impact learning outcomes, and emphasize the importance of community involvement and collaboration with colleagues. Ultimately, the goal is to provide actionable insights and reflection points that will help teachers continue to strengthen their relationships and create a positive, inclusive learning environment.

Strategies to Build Strong Relationships with Students

To build strong relationships with students both inside and outside the classroom, teachers can employ a variety of strategies that promote connection, empathy, and a positive learning environment. Here's a breakdown of key strategies for cultivating these relationships:

A. Spend time learning about them in the classroom and attend their events once in a while

One of the most effective ways to build strong connections with students is to show genuine interest in their lives. Inside the classroom, this involves asking about their interests, hobbies, and personal experiences, and weaving these into classroom discussions or activities when appropriate.

Attending students' extracurricular events—like sports games, theater performances, or art shows—demonstrates that you value them as individuals beyond their academic achievements. This personal investment shows students that you appreciate their unique talents and interests, strengthening their sense of self-worth. When students see their teacher supporting them outside the classroom, they feel truly seen, heard, and understood. This fosters a strong foundation of trust and respect, deepening the teacher-student relationship and reinforcing a positive classroom atmosphere that motivates students to engage and excel.

B. Build empathy

Empathy is a cornerstone of strong relationships in any context, and the classroom is no different. Teachers can build empathy by creating an environment where students feel safe sharing their thoughts, feelings, and experiences. Taking the time to listen actively and show understanding helps students feel supported. In practice, this could mean having open discussions about challenges students face and validating their emotions. When students know their teacher understands and cares about them, they are more likely to engage, participate, and feel motivated to succeed.

C. Parental communication/stakeholders

Maintaining open lines of communication with parents or guardians is essential for building strong relationships with students. Regularly updating parents on their child's progress, challenges, and successes creates a support system that benefits the student. This could involve sending home positive notes, scheduling regular parent-teacher conferences, or simply staying in touch through emails or phone calls. By involving parents and other stakeholders, teachers create a network of support that extends beyond the classroom, showing students that their success is a shared priority.

D. Optimistic and positive classroom community of learners

Creating an optimistic and positive classroom environment is key to promote healthy relationships built on mutual respect and encouragement. This can be achieved by setting a tone of positivity, celebrating small successes, and fostering a collaborative atmosphere where students feel encouraged to help each other. Group activities, peer learning, and open dialogue create an inclusive learning space where students feel comfortable expressing themselves. A positive classroom culture also promotes resilience, as students learn to navigate challenges with a growth mindset, knowing they are supported by both their teacher and peers.

E. Lessons that initiate team-building and fun activities with learning objectives/experiences

Incorporating team-building exercises and fun activities into the curriculum helps students bond with each other and their teacher while still working toward academic goals. These activities could include group projects, classroom games, or problem-solving challenges that require students to collaborate and communicate. Not only do these activities promote social and emotional growth, but they also help students develop critical thinking, leadership, and cooperation skills in a relaxed and enjoyable setting. By balancing fun with learning objectives, teachers can create memorable experiences that strengthen relationships and enhance the overall classroom dynamic.

Impact of Teacher-Student Relationships on Learning Outcomes

The impact of teacher-student relationships on learning outcomes is profound and multifaceted. A strong, positive relationship can be the foundation for both academic success and personal growth. Here's how various aspects of this relationship influence learning:

A. Trust and respect

When students trust and respect their teacher, they feel more comfortable taking risks in their learning. This trust allows them to ask questions, admit when they don't understand something, and actively engage in the learning process without fear of judgment. Respect for their teacher also leads to better classroom behavior, as students are more likely to follow guidelines and expectations when they feel respected in return. Trust and respect create a reciprocal relationship where learning can flourish.

B. Motivation

A strong teacher-student relationship can significantly boost a student's motivation to learn. When students feel that their teacher cares about them and believes in their potential, they are more driven to put in effort, participate actively, and persevere through challenges. Positive reinforcement, encouragement, and a teacher's belief in their abilities can inspire students to push themselves harder, leading to improved academic performance.

C. Academic success

Research shows that students who have strong relationships with their teachers tend to perform better academically. A supportive teacher creates an environment where students are more likely to stay engaged with the content, ask for help when needed, and stay focused on their goals. When students feel connected to their teacher, they are more likely to attend class regularly, complete assignments, and ultimately succeed academically.

D. Emotional safety

A nurturing teacher-student relationship provides students with a sense of emotional safety, which is crucial for learning. When students feel emotionally secure, they are better able to focus on the material being taught rather than being distracted by anxiety, stress, or fear of failure. Emotional safety allows students to open up, share their thoughts, and express themselves, leading to deeper learning and more meaningful engagement.

E. Social/emotional skills

Positive teacher-student relationships also help students develop essential social and emotional skills. Through daily interactions with a supportive teacher, students learn how to communicate effectively, manage their emotions, and navigate relationships with their peers. These skills are critical not only for academic success but also for personal development and future life challenges. Teachers model empathy, conflict resolution, and cooperation, which students can then apply in their own lives.

Here are some of the practical examples of how strong teacher-student relationships can positively influence a student's performance or attitude:

A. Attended football game of a student

There was a time when a teacher decided to attend one of her student's football games. This particular student hadn't been very engaged in class initially, but she knew he had a passion for sports. When she showed up at his game, he noticed her there, and the next day, he approached her with a big smile, saying, "I saw you there, and I won't let you down." That small gesture of taking an interest in his life beyond academics created a bridge of trust, and from that point on, his focus and participation in class significantly improved. This experience highlighted to the teacher how a bit of personal investment in a student's life could lead to greater engagement and success in the classroom.

B. Home visit

Another time, a teacher made a home visit to meet with the family of a student who had been struggling both academically and behaviorally. Sitting down in their living room, they discussed shared goals for his success, emphasizing that everyone was on the same team. For the student, it was eye-opening to see his teacher as more than just a school figure—as someone genuinely invested in his well-being and future. After that meeting, his behavior improved significantly, and he began to take his assignments more seriously. He came to understand that his teacher and family were working together as an extended support system focused on his success.

C. Individual conferences on academics/social emotional

The teacher often holds individual conferences with students to check in on both their academic progress and emotional well-being. During one of these conferences, a student who had been struggling in multiple subjects became completely transparent about their challenges once they realized the teacher wasn't solely focused on grades but also on how they were feeling and managing stress. After setting clear goals and expectations together, there was an immediate improvement in the student's performance. They became more organized, more communicative, and gained confidence in class. This personal connection helped the student feel seen and heard, motivating them to meet the expectations they had set together.

D. Student aware of norms in the class

In the classroom, the teacher ensures that students are fully aware of the norms, consequences, and transitions, providing them with a sense of structure and predictability. One student, in particular, initially struggled to adjust to this structure, but after developing a strong rapport, they began to understand the importance of these expectations. With a clearer understanding of what was expected and the consequences for their actions, the student started to take more responsibility. This strengthened relationship fostered greater self-awareness and led to improvements in both behavior and academic performance.

Key Approaches for Collaborating with Colleagues

To enhance professional growth and improve teaching practices, its important to focus on collaboration with colleagues through a few key approaches:

A. Learn from each other

The team plans collaboratively, shares their strengths, and actively seeks advice in areas where growth is needed. This approach fosters a culture of ownership and mutual learning, where everyone benefits from one another's experiences and insights.

B. Peer review

Educators often review each other's work to deepen their understanding of the subjects they teach and refine their teaching methods. This collaborative process provides valuable insights and fosters continuous improvement, helping teachers evolve and better support their students.

C. Involving other professionals

Collaboration extends beyond just teachers. Educators often work closely with administrators, counselors, social workers, and psychologists to address students' needs in a holistic way, ensuring that all aspects of a student's well-being are considered. This teamwork helps improve classroom dynamics and creates a more supportive, well-rounded learning environment.

D. Conflict resolution

Open communication is essential for maintaining a positive and supportive work environment. By addressing conflicts directly with colleagues through honest and respectful conversations, teachers can foster trust and collaboration, ensuring that any issues are resolved constructively. This approach helps build stronger relationships and a more effective team dynamic.

Insights from Educators: Improving Learning Experiences

In a series of interviews, five individuals were asked to gather their insights on how teachers can make learning more engaging and productive. Each offered unique perspectives that highlight various strategies for fostering a more effective and supportive learning environment.

Hylene Jones-Pankey

- Start the day with a warm greeting and a question about how students are feeling. This helps set a positive tone for the rest of the day.
- Make learning creative by varying teaching methods to keep students engaged.
- Integrate technology into lesson plans to make learning more interactive and relevant.
- Incorporate music and art into lessons to make them more dynamic and engaging.
- Maintain regular communication to build strong relationships with students.

Nandi Kereeletswe

- After each lesson, students should provide feedback to check for understanding and clarify concepts.
- Encourage students to communicate their preferred learning methods so that teachers can adjust their instruction accordingly.
- Emphasize the importance of asking questions, both in class and later in professional settings.

Rev. Cornell Jones

- Assess students' learning styles to tailor lessons to their individual needs.

- Take time to learn about the students' cultural backgrounds and personal experiences.
- Implement mentoring to help students learn from mistakes and focus on building their strengths.
- Attend community events to support students outside of the classroom and strengthen connections.
- Build relationships with students that go beyond discipline; ensure students know they are supported.

Dr. Sam Proctor

- Create lessons that are practical and relevant to real-life situations.
- Encourage students to embrace mistakes as part of the learning process.
- Offer emotional and academic support to foster student growth.
- Inspire students to learn something new every day, cultivating a love for learning.
- Build up students' confidence so they believe in themselves and their abilities.

Dr. Alfreda Robinson

- Provide students with options in lessons to give them a sense of ownership over their learning.

- Speak clearly and pause during lessons to check for understanding and clarify any confusion.
- Model the work you expect students to do, showing them step-by-step how to achieve success.
- Use current events and real-world examples to make lessons more relatable and engaging.
- Consult with colleagues for fresh ideas and approaches to improve lesson effectiveness.

CHAPTER 5

ADAPTABILITY AND GROWTH

Adaptability is one of the most essential qualities a teacher can possess. In today's ever-evolving educational landscape, the ability to adjust teaching methods, embrace new technologies, and continuously grow professionally is crucial for success. This chapter explores how adaptability not only enhances teaching effectiveness but also supports personal and professional growth.

Staying current with educational trends is no longer optional; it's a necessary part of being an effective educator. Whether it's integrating new technology, adopting innovative teaching techniques, or implementing research-based strategies, teachers must be lifelong learners. This chapter delves into the importance of keeping up with the latest in education through reading, professional development, and collaboration with peers.

Flexibility is another cornerstone of teaching success. Whether it's adjusting lesson plans to meet the unique needs of students or rethinking assessment methods to accommodate different learning styles, being adaptable allows teachers to reach every student. This flexibility extends beyond the classroom and into personal development, where educators must balance the demands of their professional responsibilities with their own personal growth and well-being.

In this chapter, we will explore strategies to stay adaptable and resilient in the face of change. From utilizing a variety of teaching methods to continuously refining your skills through professional development, we'll provide practical tools and resources to help you grow as both an educator and an individual. By the end of this chapter, you'll have a roadmap for navigating the evolving educational environment with confidence, and you'll reflect on your own personal growth as you continue your teaching journey.

Staying Current with Educational Trends

In the rapidly changing field of education, staying up-to-date with the latest trends is essential for effective teaching. Educators must continuously adapt and evolve to provide the best learning experiences for their students. Here are several key strategies that can help teachers stay current with educational developments:

Online Communities

Engaging with online communities allows educators to share resources, insights, and experiences with colleagues from around the world. Platforms such as discussion forums, social media groups, and professional networks provide access to a wealth of information, best practices, and new ideas. By actively participating in these communities, teachers can stay informed about the latest trends in education and exchange ideas with others in the field.

Technology Advancements and Artificial Intelligence

As technology continues to reshape education, incorporating advancements like artificial intelligence (AI) into teaching practices is becoming more crucial. AI tools can help with personalized learning, assessment, and classroom management, offering more efficiency and tailored instruction for students. Teachers who stay informed about these technologies are better equipped to integrate them into their classrooms and improve student outcomes.

Experimenting with Trial and Error Methods

Adapting to new educational trends often requires a willingness to experiment. By trying different teaching strategies, tools, and methods, educators can discover what works best for their students. This trial-and-error approach allows teachers to refine their practices, make necessary adjustments, and innovate continuously. Being open to change and learning from mistakes is key to staying adaptable and effective.

Constructive Criticism from Experts and Colleagues

Feedback from peers and educational experts is invaluable for growth. Whether it's through peer reviews, collaborative teaching, or consultations with experienced educators, constructive criticism helps teachers identify areas for improvement. This feedback loop enables them to stay aligned with current trends and refine their methods to enhance student engagement and learning.

EdTech Blogs and Podcasts

Educational technology blogs and podcasts offer a convenient way to stay updated on the latest tools, techniques, and research in the education sector. By following trusted sources, educators can gain insights into innovative teaching strategies and emerging trends. These resources often provide practical examples of how to implement new developments, helping teachers stay informed and inspired.

Engaging in Continuous Professional Development

Continuous professional development (CPD) is essential for educators who wish to refine their skills, adapt to new teaching methods, and enhance their overall effectiveness. Here's how teachers can strategically engage in CPD and ensure it positively impacts their teaching:

Active Learning and Incorporation into Lessons

Engaging in professional development should involve active learning, where educators actively participate in workshops, seminars, and courses rather than passively receiving information. By incorporating new strategies and techniques directly into their lessons, teachers can immediately apply what they've learned. This hands-on approach ensures that the professional development is relevant and directly benefits their teaching practices.

Follow-Up

To maximize the impact of professional development, follow-up is crucial. This means revisiting and reflecting on what was learned during training sessions and assessing its effectiveness in the classroom. Teachers should set specific goals for implementing new strategies, track their progress, and make adjustments as needed. Regular follow-up helps reinforce new skills and ensures they become an integral part of teaching practice.

Collaboration

Professional development is often more impactful when shared with colleagues. By collaborating with fellow educators, teachers can discuss new ideas, share insights, and provide support for implementing new strategies. Collaborative efforts can lead to a richer exchange of knowledge and create a supportive environment for trying out new techniques.

Enroll in Subject-Specific Courses

Taking specialized courses related to their subject area allows educators to deepen their expertise and stay abreast of advancements in their field. These courses provide targeted knowledge and skills that can enhance teaching effectiveness and help teachers address specific challenges related to their subject matter.

Visit Other Educational Institutions

Observing teaching practices at other educational institutions offers valuable insights into different approaches and methodologies. By visiting schools and classrooms where educators are successfully implementing innovative practices, teachers can gain inspiration and practical ideas for improving their own teaching.

Ensuring Positive Impact on Teaching

Structure Lessons

To ensure that professional development positively impacts teaching, lessons should be structured to integrate new strategies effectively. Clear organization and planning help in applying new techniques in a coherent manner, enhancing both the teaching process and student learning outcomes.

Explicit Teaching

Clear, explicit teaching involves defining learning objectives and expectations upfront. By making these elements transparent, educators can ensure that students understand the purpose of new strategies and how they fit into the overall curriculum. This clarity helps in better implementation and evaluation of professional development techniques.

Multiple Exposures

Repeated exposure to new concepts and techniques is essential for effective learning. Educators should provide multiple opportunities for students to engage with new material, which reinforces learning and helps students internalize the concepts being taught. This approach also allows teachers to refine and adjust their use of new strategies based on student feedback and outcomes.

Higher-Order Questioning Techniques

Incorporating higher-order questioning techniques, such as application, synthesis, and evaluation, encourages students to think critically and engage deeply with the material. These techniques help students apply what they've learned in meaningful ways, enhancing their understanding and retention.

Metacognitive Strategies

Teaching metacognitive strategies helps students become aware of their own learning processes. By guiding students to reflect on their thinking and problem-solving approaches, educators can foster greater self-awareness and independence in learning. This not only supports academic growth but also enhances the effectiveness of new teaching methods.

Maintaining Flexibility in Teaching Methods and Assessment Strategies

Flexibility in teaching methods and assessment strategies is crucial for addressing diverse student needs and adapting to changing classroom dynamics. Here's how educators can maintain this flexibility:

Build Relationships

Establishing strong relationships with students allows educators to better understand individual learning needs and preferences. By building trust and rapport, teachers can gain insights into what motivates and supports each student, enabling them to tailor their teaching approaches accordingly. Strong relationships also creates a positive classroom environment where students feel valued and understood.

Encourage Collaboration

Promoting collaboration among students can enhance learning experiences and accommodate various needs. Group work and collaborative projects allow students to learn from one another and leverage their diverse strengths. By encouraging collaboration, educators create opportunities for peer support and shared problem-solving, which can address different learning styles and needs effectively.

Create Different Lessons for Different Learning Styles

To meet the diverse needs of students, educators should develop lessons that cater to various learning styles, such as auditory, visual, and kinesthetic. By designing activities and materials that address different preferences, teachers ensure that all students have the opportunity to engage with the content in a way that suits them best. This approach helps in accommodating individual differences and improving overall learning outcomes.

Present Lessons in Different Formats

Offering lessons in multiple formats can enhance accessibility and engagement. For example, presenting information through lectures, multimedia, hands-on activities, and interactive discussions allows students to interact with the material in various ways. This flexibility helps to address different learning needs and keeps students engaged by providing multiple entry points to the content.

Incorporate Personal Beliefs into Lessons, but Ensure Fairness

Incorporating personal beliefs into lessons can enrich the learning experience and provide students with a broader perspective. However, it's important for educators to ensure that their beliefs do not overshadow fairness and inclusivity. Lessons should be designed to respect and acknowledge diverse viewpoints while promoting an environment where all students feel respected and valued. Balancing personal beliefs with fairness helps maintain a positive and equitable classroom atmosphere.

Balancing Professional Responsibilities with Personal Growth and Well-Being

Balancing professional responsibilities with personal growth and well-being involves strategic planning and self-care. Here's how to achieve this balance:

Time Management

Effective time management helps allocate sufficient time for both professional duties and personal activities. Prioritizing tasks and setting clear boundaries between work and personal life ensures that neither area overshadows the other.

Wellness Initiatives

Participating in wellness initiatives, such as health programs or exercise routines, supports physical and mental well-being. These practices help maintain energy levels and reduce stress, contributing to a more balanced lifestyle.

Leadership Skills

Developing leadership skills can enhance efficiency and productivity, allowing for better delegation of tasks and improved work-life balance. Strong leadership helps manage professional responsibilities more effectively.

Flexible Work Arrangements

Taking advantage of flexible work arrangements, such as remote work or adjustable hours, can help accommodate personal needs and responsibilities, making it easier to balance work and personal life.

Self-Care

Prioritizing self-care activities, such as regular relaxation and personal time, is essential for maintaining overall well-being. Self-care practices help recharge and prevent burnout.

Hobbies

Engaging in hobbies provides a creative outlet and relaxation, contributing to personal satisfaction and balance. Hobbies offer a break from professional responsibilities and promote mental wellness.

Family Time

Spending quality time with family fosters strong relationships and supports emotional well-being. Balancing professional duties with family time helps maintain a healthy personal life.

Mindfulness

Practicing mindfulness techniques, such as meditation or deep breathing, helps manage stress and maintain focus. Mindfulness contributes to mental clarity and emotional stability.

Access Priorities

Regularly assessing and adjusting priorities ensures that both professional and personal goals are met. This approach helps maintain a balanced focus and prevents one area from dominating.

Vacations

Taking vacations provides a necessary break from work and allows for relaxation and rejuvenation. Time away from professional responsibilities supports long-term productivity and personal well-being.

Supportive Network

Building a supportive network of colleagues, friends, and family provides emotional and practical support, helping to manage both professional and personal challenges effectively.

Maintain Balance

Continuously working to maintain balance between work and personal life is crucial. Regular reflection and adjustment of routines help sustain this equilibrium.

Learn to Say No

Knowing when to say no is important for managing workload and personal time effectively. Setting boundaries helps prevent overcommitment and supports a healthier balance.

Key Resources for Adaptability and Growth in Teaching

Here are some key resources that have significantly influenced approaches to adaptability and growth in teaching:

Limitless Future by Brian Butler – Encourages forward-thinking in education.

Every Student Deserves a Gifted Education by Brian Butler – Focuses on providing quality education for all students.

Ruthless Equity by Ken Williams – Explores the importance of equity in education.

The Power of You presentation by Dr. Robert Pipkin – Inspires personal empowerment and leadership.

How Children Succeed by Paul Tough – Examines the role of resilience and character in children's success.

Mindset: The New Psychology by Carol Dweck – Highlights the importance of a growth mindset.

Make it Stick by Peter C. Brown, Mark A. McDaniel – Offers insights on effective learning strategies.

CHAPTER 6

SPIRITUAL FOUNDATIONS IN TEACHING

Teaching is more than imparting knowledge; it's about nurturing the hearts and minds of students to help them grow into compassionate, resilient, and thoughtful individuals. In this chapter, we explore the often-overlooked dimension of spirituality in education—how love, faith, and hope form the backbone of a nurturing classroom environment. A spiritually grounded teacher creates a space where students feel valued and supported, not just academically, but emotionally and morally as well. Integrating spirituality into teaching fosters a holistic approach, addressing the mind and soul, and contributing to a deeper connection between teacher and student.

Spiritual foundations in teaching are not tied to a particular religion but reflect universal principles of love, empathy, patience, and understanding. These qualities create a safe and emotionally intelligent learning space where students thrive. By fostering emotional regulation and self-awareness, educators can lead by example, guiding students through their personal and academic journeys with grace and compassion. Spirituality also serves as an anchor for teachers, helping them remain focused, grounded, and resilient in the face of everyday challenges.

This chapter will delve into the use of the beatitudes—principles rooted in spiritual wisdom—as a framework for emotional regulation and daily reflection. In moments of frustration or challenge, reflecting on values such as kindness, humility, and perseverance can help both teachers and students navigate difficulties with grace. When teachers model these values, they instill the same resilience in their students, creating a positive and supportive learning environment.

Additionally, cultivating a positive attitude and mindset plays a crucial role in shaping both the teacher's and students' approach to learning. A classroom driven by optimism encourages students to believe in their abilities and stay motivated, even when faced with obstacles. By consciously integrating practices such as prayer or seeking spiritual guidance in tough situations, educators can maintain their inner strength and provide a sense of calm and stability for their students.

Throughout this chapter, we'll also share stories and reflections from educators who have successfully integrated spirituality into their teaching. These anecdotes will highlight the transformative power of a spiritual approach to education, showing how a grounded belief system can positively impact both student outcomes and teacher well-being.

The goal of this chapter is to provide teachers with tools for spiritual reflection and emotional intelligence in their teaching practices. By the end of the chapter, you will be encouraged to engage in a personal spiritual reflection exercise and create an action plan that integrates love, faith, and hope into your teaching journey. This approach not only enriches the lives of students but also nurtures the well-being of the teacher, creating a balanced and harmonious educational experience.

Love

Trust: Trust is the cornerstone of any strong relationship, and this is especially true in a classroom. Building trust with students takes time, consistency, and genuine effort. By creating an open and welcoming environment, teachers can make students feel valued and understood. When students feel trusted, they are more likely to take risks in their learning and open up about their challenges. It fosters a sense of security that allows them to engage deeply in the educational process. Trust can be established through honest communication, keeping promises, and showing consistent support.

Vulnerability: As a teacher, being vulnerable means demonstrating that making mistakes is a natural part of the learning process. When teachers openly acknowledge their own errors and show how they correct them, it teaches students that failure isn't something to fear but an opportunity for growth. This vulnerability helps to humanize the teacher and encourages students to be more accepting of their own mistakes. Leading by example, teachers show that growth comes from perseverance and reflection, not perfection.

Empathy: Empathy in the classroom is about taking the time to understand students' feelings and needs. By listening attentively and responding with compassion, teachers validate students' experiences and emotions. This emotional connection fosters a classroom environment where students feel understood and supported. Empathetic teachers take the time to notice when students are struggling, offering help or guidance before things escalate. Being slow to speak and quick to listen can diffuse tension, build trust, and strengthen relationships.

Inclusion: Inclusion goes beyond simply allowing students to participate. It's about giving them a sense of ownership in their learning journey. By involving students in decision-making processes and tailoring learning experiences to their preferences, teachers help students feel empowered. Giving students a voice in the classroom not only fosters engagement but also instills a sense of responsibility for their learning. When students feel included, they are more likely to take initiative and feel invested in their success.

Patience: Patience is crucial in teaching. Students learn at different paces, and some may need extra time or support to grasp concepts. Teachers who show patience, both with the material and the students, create an environment where students feel supported, not rushed or judged. Being patient allows teachers to encourage students through their struggles rather than expecting immediate mastery. This understanding approach fosters a growth mindset, where students feel that improvement comes through effort, not simply inherent ability.

Faith

Demonstrating Belief: Teachers can demonstrate the power of belief by showing how persistence, self-belief, and resilience lead to success. By sharing stories of perseverance, either personal or from others, teachers inspire students to keep going even when things seem difficult. Teachers can model faith by believing in their students' potential and showing them that with dedication, they can overcome challenges. This can be particularly impactful for students who struggle with self-confidence, helping them develop a stronger sense of belief in themselves.

Persistence: Faith isn't just about believing without evidence—it's about trusting that hard work and persistence will lead to improvement. Teachers can cultivate this belief in their students by reinforcing the idea that effort leads to growth. When students face obstacles, teachers can encourage them to keep trying, emphasizing that success doesn't always come easily, but with persistence, it will come. This helps students develop a strong sense of faith in their own abilities and in the value of hard work.

Ethical Dilemmas: Presenting ethical dilemmas or moral challenges to students helps them develop faith in their own moral compass. When faced with tough decisions, teachers can guide students through reflective discussions on right and wrong, showing that faith in one's values is important for navigating life's challenges. By allowing students to express their beliefs and views in a safe environment, teachers encourage them to trust their instincts and the importance of standing by their principles.

Believing Without Seeing: Teachers can show students that sometimes, belief comes before visible evidence. Just as many people believe in things they cannot see (such as hope for the future, or love for others), teachers can emphasize that belief is not always about proof but about trust in the process. This can be empowering for students who may feel they cannot accomplish something right now. They can learn to trust that with continued effort, the results will come.

Hope

Goal Setting: Hope is rooted in the belief that the future holds positive possibilities. Teachers can help students cultivate hope by guiding them in setting meaningful goals. When students set clear, achievable goals, they develop a sense of purpose and direction. This forward-thinking approach encourages students to focus on what they can achieve rather than being bogged down by present challenges. Teachers can facilitate goal setting by breaking down large goals into smaller, manageable steps, which helps students stay motivated and hopeful about their progress.

Classroom Ownership: Hope grows when students feel that they have control over their own learning. Teachers can foster hope by encouraging students to take ownership of their education. By involving students in decision-making processes regarding their learning path, teachers empower them to believe in their own abilities. Students who have agency in their education are more likely to feel motivated and hopeful because they believe they can influence their success.

Scenarios of Hope: Sharing real-life scenarios where hope made a difference can help students see the power of optimism. Teachers can present stories of individuals who overcame significant obstacles to achieve success. By seeing examples of perseverance, students are reminded that challenges are temporary and that hope can guide them through difficult times. These scenarios help students understand that hope is not passive but an active force that drives positive outcomes.

Success Stories: Teachers can share stories of people who came from challenging backgrounds and achieved success. These examples help students see that no matter where they come from, their circumstances do not dictate their future. By showing how hope, determination, and effort lead to success, teachers inspire students to pursue their own dreams despite obstacles. This instills in students a sense of belief that they, too, can overcome adversity and achieve their goals.

Impact on Students

Sense of Purpose: Incorporating love, faith, and hope into teaching gives students a sense of purpose, helping them see the importance of their education and the potential impact they can have on the world. When students know that their teachers believe in them and their ability to succeed, they feel a sense of responsibility to make the most of their opportunities.

Broader Perspective: Students exposed to love, faith, and hope are more likely to develop a broader perspective on life. They learn to appreciate the value of empathy, persistence, and optimism, which extends beyond the classroom and into their personal lives. This broader worldview helps them approach life with confidence and understanding.

Spiritual/Emotional Beliefs: Spiritual foundations provide students with a deeper connection to their own values and beliefs.

When students are encouraged to reflect on their emotions and spirituality, they become more self-aware and emotionally intelligent. This emotional grounding helps them navigate challenges and conflicts with a sense of inner peace and understanding.

Social/Emotional Development: Teachers who model love, faith, and hope foster students' social and emotional development. Students learn how to interact with others, manage their emotions, and build healthy relationships. These skills are essential for their academic success and personal well-being.

Leadership: The positive environment created by love, faith, and hope encourages students to take on leadership roles in the classroom. They develop a sense of responsibility and a desire to support their peers, making them more likely to step up as leaders in various contexts.

Encouragement and Transformation: Teachers who embody these qualities provide students with the encouragement they need to believe in themselves and their potential. This support can be transformational, helping students overcome self-doubt and unlock their full potential. When students feel loved, supported, and hopeful, they are more likely to succeed, both academically and in life.

Using the Beatitudes for Emotional Regulation

Daily Focus: The beatitudes serve as a daily guide, offering reminders throughout the day to practice kindness, humility, and patience. At the end of each day, reflecting on how these values were implemented helps create accountability and demonstrates the positive impact they had on others.

Blueprint of Peace, Acceptance, and Happiness: The beatitudes provide a foundational framework for living with peace, acceptance, and happiness. They help teachers maintain emotional balance in challenging situations, creating a harmonious classroom environment.

Foundation for Structuring the Day: By using the beatitudes as a foundation, teachers can structure their day around principles of compassion, understanding, and empathy, which influence their interactions with students and colleagues.

Fostering a Positive Attitude and Mindset

1. **Practice Gratitude**: Incorporating gratitude into the classroom can have a profound impact on students' well-being. Encourage students to start or end each day by sharing something they are grateful for. This simple practice can shift their focus from challenges to positive aspects of their lives, fostering a more positive and resilient classroom environment.

2. **Set SMART Goals**: Helping students set SMART goals provides them with clear direction and a sense of purpose. By ensuring that their goals are Specific, Measurable, Achievable, Relevant, and Time-bound, students are more likely to stay motivated and focused. These goals help them track progress, celebrate small wins, and remain engaged in their learning.
3. **Celebrate Success**: Celebrating both big and small victories reinforces positive behaviors and boosts students' confidence. Acknowledging achievements in front of peers, whether academic or personal, promotes a growth-focused culture and motivates students to keep striving for success. This practice nurtures a sense of accomplishment and belonging in the classroom.
4. **Association and Simulation**: Using real-life examples and role-playing activities connects classroom lessons to students' lives and experiences. By simulating real-world scenarios, students gain a deeper understanding of the material and can better relate to its practical applications. This fosters an environment where learning is not just theoretical but tied to personal growth and problem-solving skills.
5. **Embrace Challenges**: Encouraging students to view challenges as opportunities for growth cultivates resilience. When faced with obstacles, students who see them as learning experiences are more likely to persist and overcome setbacks. This mindset

helps them develop a deeper understanding that effort, rather than avoidance, leads to improvement.

6. **Positive Self-Affirmations**: Teaching students to use positive self-talk helps to build their self-esteem and confidence. Encourage them to repeat affirmations such as "I can improve with practice" or "Mistakes help me grow." This simple tool can empower students to believe in their ability to succeed and approach challenges with a more optimistic attitude.

7. **Growth Mindset**: A growth mindset encourages students to understand that intelligence is not fixed but can be developed through effort and perseverance. By praising effort over innate talent, teachers can help students embrace challenges, see mistakes as part of the learning process, and stay motivated through difficulties.

8. **Build Each Other Up**: Fostering an environment where students support one another builds a strong sense of community in the classroom. Encouraging peer feedback, collaborative projects, and positive reinforcement creates an atmosphere where students feel safe to express themselves, take risks, and help each other succeed.

9. **Encourage and Create Value**: Consistently encouraging students by recognizing their potential and reinforcing their value helps them feel seen and appreciated. Highlighting their strengths, both in and out of the classroom, boosts their self-

worth and motivates them to contribute more to the classroom community. This recognition can foster a sense of pride and drive in students.

Role of a Positive Attitude and Mindset in Learning

Enduring Knowledge and Real-World Application: Cultivating a positive mindset helps students retain information more effectively, making it applicable beyond the classroom. This kind of mindset fosters lifelong learning and prepares students for the challenges they'll face in the workforce, where problem-solving, collaboration, and adaptability are essential.

Builds Confidence and Stamina: A positive attitude equips students with the self-belief to tackle difficult tasks without fear of failure. It encourages them to persevere through challenges, knowing that effort leads to growth. As they experience success through hard work, their confidence increases, and they build the mental stamina to face more complex challenges in the future.

Improves Communication Skills: A positive classroom environment encourages open and respectful dialogue. When students feel valued and confident, they are more willing to share their thoughts, ask questions, and engage in discussions. This not only enhances their communication skills but also fosters a collaborative learning experience where ideas can be exchanged freely, leading to deeper understanding and innovation.

Role of Spiritual Guidance in Navigating Teaching Challenges

1. **Students with Learning Difficulties**: Prayer can provide teachers with the patience and clarity needed to approach students with diverse learning needs. It helps educators focus on students' strengths rather than their challenges, encouraging them to adapt their methods, offer additional support, and create a nurturing environment where students feel capable and supported.

2. **Behavior Problems (Discipline)**: In dealing with behavioral issues, many teachers seek spiritual guidance to maintain a calm and compassionate demeanor. Rather than reacting in frustration, they pray for wisdom to understand the underlying causes of the behavior and respond with empathy. This approach focuses on constructive correction and relationship-building rather than punitive measures.

3. **Difficult Colleagues (Gaslighting)**: When dealing with toxic dynamics, such as gaslighting from colleagues, many educators turn to prayer for strength and clarity. It helps them stay grounded, clear-minded, and self-assured, preventing emotional entanglements. Through spiritual reflection, they seek the strength to address such issues professionally while maintaining their integrity.

4. **Overwhelming Schedule, Meetings, and Workshops**: When the workload feels overwhelming, prayer helps educators center

themselves and focus on what truly matters. It provides guidance in prioritizing tasks, balancing professional demands with personal well-being, and approaching each challenge with peace and purpose.

Spiritual Practices and Anecdotes that Shaped My Approach to Teaching

1. **Being Flexible with Lessons**: One time, I meticulously planned what I thought was a great lesson, but it completely flopped because my students weren't in the right state of mind. Many were dealing with personal issues at home, and no amount of instruction would have resonated that day. I realized the moral of the situation: sometimes, you need to pause the curriculum and focus on the students' well-being. Instead of teaching the planned lesson, we had an open, heartfelt chat. That day taught me that being flexible and human often matters more than sticking rigidly to a lesson plan.

2. **Quality Over Quantity**: It's not about how long or complex a lesson is but whether students truly understand and engage with it. This understanding shifted my focus to prioritizing student learning and comprehension over the amount of content covered. It made me more attuned to their needs and more intentional with my teaching.

3. **Instilling Belief in Students**: A significant part of my teaching philosophy is helping students believe in themselves. By consistently encouraging them and showing faith in their abilities, I've seen even the most hesitant students begin to thrive. This belief-building has had a profound effect on their confidence, transforming not only their academic success but also their sense of self-worth.

4. **Showing Vulnerability**: I've learned to embrace my humanity in the classroom. Letting students see that I'm not perfect—that I make mistakes just like they do—helps break down barriers. It shows them that learning is a lifelong process, and it's okay not to have all the answers. This vulnerability has deepened my connection with students and created an environment of mutual respect and understanding.

5. **Consistency in Character**: While flexibility is key, being consistent in my expectations, responses, and character is just as crucial. Students need to know that I am dependable and that the classroom is a stable, safe space. Striving for consistency helps build trust and respect, which are the foundation of any strong student-teacher relationship.

Impact of Spiritual Practices on Teacher-Student Relationships

These spiritual practices have significantly deepened my relationship with students.

1. **Students understand that they are human and can make mistakes**: By showing my own vulnerability, they learn that making mistakes is part of the learning process, and it takes the pressure off striving for perfection.
2. **Students learn that asking questions means they are smart, not dumb**: Creating an environment where questions are encouraged has taught students that curiosity is a sign of intelligence and that seeking clarity is a valuable skill, not a weakness.
3. **Students are more comfortable and are encouraged to think critically**: With this openness, students feel safer and more confident, which encourages them to engage in meaningful, critical thinking. It creates a space where they're not just absorbing information but actively processing and questioning it.

CHAPTER 7
OVERCOMING CHALLENGES

Teaching is a rewarding yet demanding profession, often filled with unique obstacles that require resilience, creativity, and perseverance. This chapter explores common challenges teachers face and offers practical strategies for navigating them effectively. From managing time and limited resources to handling large class sizes and absenteeism, educators must be adaptable and resourceful in finding solutions that benefit both students and themselves. Balancing professional responsibilities with maintaining mental health and well-being is essential for long-term success in the field. Through testimonials from experienced teachers, we'll dive into real-world examples of how they've tackled these challenges head-on, and reflect on strategies for overcoming them. This chapter aims to empower educators with problem-solving skills and a renewed sense of purpose, while offering a reflective guide to help address personal challenges along the way.

Strategies for Effective Time Management and Resource Budgeting in Teaching

In a teaching environment characterized by limited support, effective time management and resource budgeting are essential for creating a productive and enriching learning atmosphere. Here are some strategies to consider:

Time Management Strategies

1. **Prioritize Important Tasks**: Focus on tasks that have the greatest impact on student learning and classroom success. Use a prioritization matrix to determine what requires immediate attention versus what can wait.

2. **Learn to Delegate/Outsource**: Engage students or enlist the help of colleagues for specific tasks, such as classroom organization or project assistance. This not only lightens your load but also fosters a collaborative environment.

3. **Organize Schedule/Routines**: Establish a structured routine that includes dedicated time for lesson planning, grading, and student engagement. Tools like planners or digital calendars can help keep you on track.

4. **Pace Yourself and Set Goal Limits**: Break down larger tasks into manageable chunks and set realistic deadlines. This prevents burnout and ensures consistent progress throughout the school year.

5. **Deal with Stress Wisely**: Incorporate stress-management techniques such as mindfulness, exercise, or taking breaks to maintain your well-being, allowing you to be more focused and effective in the classroom.

Budgeting Resources Strategies

1. **Apply for Grants**: Research and apply for educational grants to secure additional funding for classroom materials and activities. This can significantly alleviate financial constraints.
2. **Use Existing Materials**: Make the most of materials you already have. Get creative with repurposing supplies and resources to develop engaging lessons without additional costs.
3. **Manage County Donations vs. Out-of-Pocket Spending**: Keep track of resources available through your school district and manage personal expenses wisely. Seek donations from local businesses to supplement classroom needs.
4. **Go Paperless**: Reduce paper usage by implementing digital assignments and resources. This not only saves money but also supports an environmentally friendly approach.
5. **Alternative Resources**: Explore low-cost or free educational resources online. Platforms like Khan Academy or Teachers Pay Teachers offer valuable materials that can enhance your lessons without breaking the bank.

Strategies for Addressing Large Class Sizes and Limited Resources

Managing large class sizes and limited resources can be daunting for educators, but with strategic approaches, it's possible to ensure that each student receives the attention and support they need. Here are effective strategies to consider:

Addressing Large Class Sizes

1. **Set Clearly Defined Limits and Expectations**: Establish clear behavioral and academic expectations from the outset. Communicate these guidelines consistently to help create a structured environment where students understand what is required of them.
2. **Follow Routines and Model Them Consistently**: Implement and maintain consistent routines that facilitate classroom management. By modeling these routines, students will know what to expect and can transition smoothly between activities.
3. **Adjust Lesson Plans to Fit Different Learning Styles**: Recognize that students have varying learning preferences. Modify lesson plans to incorporate diverse teaching methods—such as visual aids, hands-on activities, and group discussions—to engage all learners effectively.
4. **Assess and Check Individually, with Whole Group, and in Cooperative Groups**: Utilize a mix of assessment strategies to

gauge understanding. Conduct individual assessments, lead whole-group discussions, and encourage cooperative learning to ensure that each student's needs are met.

5. **Ongoing Activities That Require Movement and Hands-On Lessons**: Integrate activities that promote movement and active participation. Hands-on lessons not only keep students engaged but also cater to different learning styles, helping them absorb information more effectively.

Strategies for Addressing Absenteeism and Ensuring Student Safety

Effectively managing absenteeism and ensuring student safety are essential components of maintaining a productive learning environment. Here are key strategies that educators can implement to address these challenges:

Handling Absenteeism

1. **Keep Stakeholders in the Loop**: Maintain open lines of communication with students, parents, and school administrators regarding attendance. Regular updates can help keep everyone informed about student progress and the importance of consistent attendance.
2. **Build Relationships with Parents**: Establish strong relationships with parents to encourage their involvement in their children's education. Engaging parents fosters a supportive

home environment that emphasizes the value of attending school regularly.
3. **Use Technology and Integrate Multimedia Resources into Lessons**: Make lessons more engaging by incorporating technology and multimedia resources. Interactive tools can capture students' attention and encourage them to attend, even if they may be struggling with motivation.
4. **Mentorship Program**: Implement a mentorship program where students can receive guidance and support from teachers or peers. This program can help students feel more connected to the school community and reduce absenteeism by addressing any underlying issues they may face.
5. **Organize Regular Meetings Involving Parents**: Host meetings that include parents to discuss attendance issues and share strategies for supporting their children. Collaborative discussions can foster a sense of community and accountability.

Ensuring Student Safety

1. **Emergency Management Plan**: Develop and implement a comprehensive emergency management plan that outlines procedures for various emergencies, ensuring that all staff and students are prepared.
2. **Secure Learning Environment**: Create a secure learning environment by ensuring proper access controls, surveillance,

and maintenance of the school premises. A safe physical environment allows students to focus on their learning.
3. **Staff Training and Awareness**: Provide ongoing training for staff on safety protocols and emergency procedures. Awareness among staff members is crucial for effectively managing potential safety issues.
4. **Access Control Systems**: Utilize access control systems to monitor who enters and exits the school premises. This enhances security and helps keep unauthorized individuals from accessing the school environment.
5. **Bullying Prevention Sessions with Intervention Techniques**: Conduct sessions on bullying prevention and establish intervention techniques. Creating a culture of respect and inclusivity can help ensure that all students feel safe and valued in the school setting.

Maintaining Mental Health and Well-Being in Teaching

In the face of the unique stressors associated with the teaching profession, maintaining mental health and well-being is essential for educators. Here are some effective strategies:

1. Self-Care

Engaging in self-care activities, such as hobbies and personal interests, is crucial for managing stress. Taking time to reward oneself for accomplishments—big or small—fosters a positive mindset and promotes relaxation. Prioritizing self-care ensures that educators can recharge and approach their work with renewed energy.

2. Communicate with Loved Ones

Open communication with family and friends provides a vital support system for teachers. Sharing experiences and feelings can help alleviate stress and foster a sense of connection. Loved ones can offer encouragement, advice, and perspective, making it easier for educators to navigate challenges.

3. Healthy Work/Life Balance

Establishing a healthy work/life balance is essential for mental well-being. Setting boundaries around work hours and making time for personal interests, family, and relaxation can help prevent burnout. Educators should strive to create a schedule that allows for both professional responsibilities and personal fulfillment.

4. Work Smart

Focusing on efficiency and organization can significantly reduce stress. This involves prioritizing tasks, using technology to streamline processes, and seeking out resources that simplify lesson planning and grading. Working smart allows teachers to maximize their effectiveness while minimizing the strain of overwhelming workloads.

5. Don't Take Everything Personally

Teaching can be emotionally taxing, especially when facing challenges from students, colleagues, or parents. It's important for educators to remember that not every situation reflects their abilities or efforts. By maintaining perspective and not taking things personally, teachers can reduce stress and maintain a more balanced emotional state.

Testimonials from Educators on Overcoming Challenges

1. Creating a Structured Schedule

One educator found that implementing a structured schedule transformed her teaching experience. By clearly outlining daily tasks and adhering to a routine, she managed her time more effectively. This approach helped her prioritize responsibilities and allocate time for both teaching and self-care, reducing stress levels and fostering a more organized classroom environment.

2. Partnership with the Community

Another teacher emphasized the significance of community involvement in overcoming challenges. Building partnerships with local businesses and organizations proved to be a game-changer for her school. By launching programs that connect students with community resources, such as mentorship and internships, the school enriched its curriculum and provided real-world experiences.

This support lifted some of the burdens caused by limited resources and increased student engagement.

3. Asking for Constructive Criticism

A veteran educator highlighted the value of seeking feedback from peers. Early in his career, he struggled with teaching methods and felt uncertain about his impact. He reached out to experienced educators for constructive criticism, which proved invaluable. Embracing this feedback enhanced his teaching and built his confidence. He now collaborates regularly with colleagues to share ideas and improve practices.

CHAPTER 8

EMOTIONAL AND SOCIAL INTELLIGENCE

In the ever-changing landscape of education, emotional and social intelligence have become essential components of effective teaching. The ability to understand, regulate, and channel emotions not only enhances a teacher's ability to engage with students but also fosters a learning environment where students feel supported, valued, and understood. In this chapter, we explore how emotional intelligence can be the key to unlocking deeper connections with students, colleagues, and the wider school community.

Developing emotional intelligence begins with recognizing and regulating one's own emotions. Teachers are often faced with stressful situations, whether it's managing large class sizes, addressing behavioral challenges, or balancing administrative tasks. By cultivating emotional self-awareness, educators can remain calm under pressure, model positive emotional behavior, and create a safe space where students feel encouraged to express their own feelings.

Beyond managing emotions, building empathy and understanding within the classroom is essential. Empathy allows teachers to see the world from their students' perspectives, addressing their unique challenges and needs. By fostering this mutual understanding, teachers can create a sense of community and belonging in their classrooms, which enhances students' social and emotional development.

Communication is at the heart of emotional intelligence, and it extends beyond academic instruction. Effective communication with students and stakeholders—such as parents, caregivers, and colleagues—requires emotional sensitivity and an understanding of diverse backgrounds and perspectives. This chapter provides strategies for improving communication skills that foster trust, transparency, and collaboration.

To support educators in applying these principles, we will introduce practical tools, such as emotional intelligence exercises and strategies for improving classroom communication. By reflecting on their emotional intelligence and building it over time, teachers can enhance not only their teaching effectiveness but also the long-term success and well-being of their students.

Recognizing and Regulating Emotions in the Classroom:

1. **Create a positive classroom culture:** Foster a supportive environment where students feel safe to express their emotions.

2. Provide emotional support: Offer guidance and reassurance to students when they face emotional challenges.

3. Teach students to distract themselves: Introduce simple coping mechanisms to help them manage difficult emotions.

4. Educate students about the language of emotions: Encourage students to name and describe their feelings to build emotional awareness.

5. Mindfulness techniques: Incorporate breathing exercises and meditation to help students stay calm and focused.

6. Positive reinforcement and optimistic attitude: Reinforce positive behaviors and model a constructive outlook.

7. Calming corner or room: Create a designated space with emotional regulation tools like emotion charts and calming activities.

8. Using anchors: Allow brief activities, like listening to music or phone use, as positive incentives to manage emotions.

9. Redirection: Offer alternative activities or topics to help students cool off and refocus.

10. Cognitive appraisals: Teach students to reframe negative thoughts, fostering resilience and emotional well-being.

Strategies to Build Empathy and Understanding Among Students:

1. Model empathy: Demonstrate compassionate behavior in your interactions to show students how to empathize with others.

2. Encourage active listening: Teach students to listen attentively to understand others' viewpoints fully.

3. Encourage perspective conversations: Foster discussions where students listen and learn from differing perspectives.

4. Promote kindness: Reinforce acts of kindness to cultivate a supportive classroom environment.

5. Role play: Use role-playing activities to help students experience situations from another person's perspective.

6. Be understanding: Show patience and understanding in response to student concerns and emotions.

7. Build self-awareness: Guide students in recognizing their own feelings and how they affect others.

8. Ask open-ended questions: Use open-ended questions to encourage deeper thought and meaningful dialogue.

9. Mindfulness practice activities: Incorporate mindfulness exercises to help students become more aware of their emotions and reactions.

Strategies to Foster a Sense of Community and Belonging for All Students:

1. Getting to know students individually: Build personal relationships by learning about each student's background, interests, and needs.

2. Create opportunities for sharing: Encourage students to share their experiences and ideas to strengthen connections.

3. Cooperative learning: Promote group activities where students work together, fostering teamwork and collaboration.

4. Positive classroom climate: Establish an environment that feels safe, welcoming, and inclusive for everyone.

5. Culturally relevant curriculum: Incorporate diverse materials and perspectives that resonate with students' experiences.

6. Building community rituals: Create classroom traditions that unite students, such as weekly reflections or celebrations.

7. Give students ownership in the classroom: Allow students to have a say in classroom decisions and responsibilities.

8. Physical classroom design: Arrange the classroom to encourage interaction and create a comfortable learning space.

9. Feedback and regular meetings: Hold one-on-one and group meetings to check in with students and build rapport.

10. Open communication: Foster transparency and dialogue between students and teachers to ensure everyone feels heard.

11. Establish classroom norms: Set clear expectations and address exclusionary behaviors to promote inclusion and respect.

Communication Strategies to Enhance Interactions with Students and Stakeholders:

1. Active listening: Pay close attention to what others are saying, showing empathy and understanding in conversations.

2. Feedback: Provide constructive, timely feedback to help students and stakeholders improve and stay informed.

3. Keeping stakeholders in the loop: Regularly update parents, administrators, and others on important classroom developments and student progress.

4. Encourage teamwork: Foster collaboration by facilitating open communication and cooperation between students, parents, and staff.

5. Understanding audience: Tailor your communication style based on who you are addressing, ensuring clarity and appropriateness.

6. Conflict resolution: Address disagreements or misunderstandings calmly and fairly to maintain positive relationships.

CHAPTER 9

TOOLS FOR CONTINUED SUCCESS

In teaching, the journey toward success is continuous and ever-evolving. Chapter 9 focuses on equipping educators with practical tools and strategies to sustain their progress, grow as professionals, and make a lasting impact on their students. The goal is to streamline your work, making it more effective without overburdening yourself—working smart, not hard.

This chapter begins by offering lesson planning templates and checklists to simplify the preparation process, ensuring that each class is structured and purposeful. These templates help to break down larger tasks into manageable steps, giving teachers a clear roadmap for their daily and weekly lessons. Next, we explore tools for tracking student progress, which are essential for identifying areas of improvement and celebrating successes. With data-driven insights, educators can tailor their instruction to meet individual student needs more effectively.

We'll also dive into strategies for maintaining student engagement and fostering a positive classroom environment. The key to a thriving learning space is ensuring that students remain curious, motivated, and supported. Methods to keep lessons interactive and personalized will be explored, as well as tips on creating an atmosphere where both students and teachers can flourish.

Another critical aspect of this chapter is the development and refinement of teaching modes and methods. As classrooms evolve, so must the techniques and strategies educators use. You'll learn how to adapt your teaching styles to meet the diverse needs of learners while maintaining consistency in quality and effectiveness.

To bring these strategies to life, the chapter will include anecdotes that demonstrate the power of smart work over hard work. These real-life examples highlight how efficiency and thoughtful planning can transform challenges into opportunities for growth, benefiting both teachers and students.

Lesson Planning Templates and Checklists

ClickUp Class Planning Template

This is a versatile, project management tool that helps educators organize lessons by creating tasks, subtasks, and deadlines. Teachers can track progress, set reminders, and prioritize lessons for smoother planning. It also integrates with other tools, making collaboration and customization easy.

Google Docs

Google Docs provides a simple, collaborative platform for lesson planning. Educators can create, share, and edit lesson plans in real-time with colleagues. It's cloud-based, allowing easy access to your documents anywhere, and integrates seamlessly with other Google Workspace tools.

Teachers Pay Teachers

This resource-rich platform offers ready-made lesson planning templates from experienced teachers. It saves time by providing a wide variety of customizable templates for different subjects and grade levels. Educators can also sell and share their own plans.

Edutopia's Practice Picker Checklist

Edutopia offers a checklist that helps teachers choose evidence-based teaching strategies. This tool aids in selecting practices that align with learning objectives, ensuring that lessons are efficient and impactful. It encourages reflective practice and thoughtful planning.

Lesson Bud

Lesson Bud offers an intuitive interface where teachers can create and share lesson plans. Its tools are designed to promote engagement and interactive learning, and the platform offers access to resources like lesson templates and educational materials.

5E Lesson Plan

The 5E model (Engage, Explore, Explain, Elaborate, Evaluate) provides a structured approach to lesson planning. It encourages inquiry-based learning, guiding students from understanding concepts to applying them. This method is particularly effective for STEM subjects but adaptable across disciplines.

Tools for Tracking Student Progress

Formative Assessments

Formative assessments, such as quizzes, polls, and exit tickets, provide ongoing feedback on student understanding. They help teachers identify areas where students may be struggling, allowing for timely interventions. This approach promotes a growth mindset by focusing on progress rather than just grades.

Standardized Exams

Standardized exams offer a way to measure student performance against consistent benchmarks. They provide data on student achievement across various demographics and help inform curriculum adjustments. However, they should be balanced with other assessment types to capture a comprehensive view of student learning.

Learning Management Systems (LMS)

LMS platforms like Google Classroom and Canvas streamline the tracking of student progress by organizing assignments, grades, and feedback in one place. They offer analytics features that allow teachers to monitor student engagement and performance over time, facilitating personalized support.

Data Visualization Tools

Data visualization tools, such as Google Data Studio or Tableau, transform complex data sets into easy-to-understand visuals. They help educators analyze trends in student performance and identify strengths and weaknesses, enabling data-driven decisions to enhance instruction and accountability.

Student Self-Assessment

Encouraging students to engage in self-assessment fosters ownership of their learning. Tools like reflective journals or self-rating scales help students evaluate their understanding and set personal goals. This practice promotes accountability and encourages metacognitive skills, enabling students to take charge of their educational journey.

Maintaining Learning Atmosphere and Engagement

Get to Know Your Students

Building strong relationships with students is foundational for engagement. Taking the time to learn about their interests, strengths, and challenges fosters trust and a sense of belonging, making students more willing to participate and contribute in class.

Engaging Curriculum Design

Creating a curriculum that is relevant and interesting to students enhances engagement. Incorporating varied instructional methods, such as project-based learning, hands-on activities, and technology, keeps lessons dynamic and tailored to different learning styles.

Uplifting Classroom Scenarios

Establishing a positive and supportive classroom environment encourages student participation. This can include celebrating successes, creating a culture of respect, and using humor to lighten the mood, which helps students feel comfortable expressing themselves.

Effective Feedback and Checking for Student Understanding

Providing timely and constructive feedback is crucial for student growth. Regularly checking for understanding through formative assessments allows teachers to address misconceptions promptly and adjust instruction as needed, fostering a responsive learning environment.

Address Individual Needs

Recognizing and accommodating diverse learning needs is essential for maintaining engagement. Differentiating instruction and providing personalized support ensures that all students can participate meaningfully, contributing to a more inclusive atmosphere.

Promote Active Learning and Relate to Real-Life Situations

Encouraging students to actively participate in their learning, through discussions, group work, and problem-solving, enhances engagement. Relating lessons to real-life scenarios makes learning more relevant and applicable, sparking students' curiosity and interest.

Strategies to Develop and Refine Teaching Methods

Artificial Intelligence

Incorporating artificial intelligence tools can enhance teaching effectiveness by providing personalized learning experiences. These tools can analyze student data to identify areas for improvement, recommend resources, and automate administrative tasks, allowing educators to focus more on instruction.

Flipped Classroom

The flipped classroom model involves students learning new content at home (often through videos) and engaging in hands-on activities during class time. This approach encourages students to take ownership of their learning while allowing teachers to facilitate deeper understanding through guided practice.

Collaborative Learning

Facilitating collaborative learning encourages students to work together to solve problems and complete projects. This strategy not only fosters communication and teamwork skills but also allows students to learn from one another, enhancing their understanding of the material.

Inquiry-Based Learning

Inquiry-based learning focuses on student-led exploration and investigation of questions or problems. By encouraging curiosity and critical thinking, educators can help students develop deeper understanding and retention of concepts, making learning more meaningful and engaging.

Individual and Group Learning Sessions

Balancing individual and group learning sessions allows educators to cater to diverse learning preferences. Individual sessions enable personalized attention, while group activities promote social skills and collective problem-solving, creating a well-rounded learning experience.

Blended Learning

Blended learning combines traditional face-to-face instruction with online learning elements. This flexible approach allows educators to customize their teaching methods, offering students a mix of direct interaction and independent study that caters to varied learning styles.

Project-Based Learning

Project-based learning engages students in real-world projects that require critical thinking, collaboration, and creativity. This hands-on approach allows students to apply their knowledge in practical ways, deepening their understanding and making learning relevant to their lives.

ANECDOTE

An effective strategy for achieving teaching success is to work in short bursts followed by brief breaks. This approach not only helps maintain concentration but also prevents burnout. By prioritizing tasks and breaking them into manageable segments, educators can manage their time more efficiently, leading to greater productivity and a more sustainable work routine. For example, during a particularly hectic week filled with lesson planning and grading, I found that setting a timer for focused work sessions of 25 minutes allowed me to tackle each task with renewed energy. After a short five-minute break, I returned to my work feeling refreshed and ready to dive back in. This method transformed my productivity and helped me maintain a balanced workload, ultimately leading to a more fulfilling teaching experience.

CHAPTER 10

CREATING A LASTING IMPACT

In the rapidly evolving landscape of education, teachers hold a profound responsibility not only to impart knowledge but also to inspire and empower their students. Chapter 10, "Creating a Lasting Impact," delves into the essential qualities that define impactful educators—adaptability, spiritual development, and a commitment to fostering a culture of lifelong learning. This chapter invites educators to reflect on their unique roles in shaping the minds and hearts of future generations, encouraging them to embrace change and growth both personally and professionally.

As we explore the significance of adaptability, we will consider how teachers can navigate the challenges of an ever-changing educational environment while remaining responsive to the diverse needs of their students. Spiritual development will also be examined, highlighting the importance of fostering a sense of purpose, connection, and resilience in both teachers and students. By cultivating an atmosphere where learning is seen as a lifelong journey, educators can inspire their students to embrace curiosity and self-discovery long after they leave the classroom.

Furthermore, we will reflect on the long-term impact of effective teaching practices, emphasizing the profound influence teachers have on their students' futures and the broader education system. This chapter serves as both a call to action and a guide for educators looking to make a meaningful difference in the lives of their students. Through practical strategies and reflective exercises, readers will be equipped to design a personal action plan, ensuring their teaching journey continues to evolve and inspire, leaving a legacy that resonates for years to come.

Demonstrating Adaptability and Spiritual Development in Teaching Practices

1. Adaptability

Differentiate Instruction

Differentiating instruction involves tailoring teaching methods and materials to accommodate the diverse learning needs, interests, and abilities of students. By employing various strategies, such as flexible grouping, varied assignments, and personalized learning experiences, teachers can ensure that all students engage with the content in a way that resonates with them. This adaptability fosters a more inclusive classroom environment where every student feels valued and capable of succeeding. For instance, a teacher might offer advanced reading materials for gifted students while providing more supportive resources for those who struggle, thus meeting each learner at their individual level.

Be Open to Feedback

Being receptive to feedback is a crucial aspect of adaptability in teaching. This means actively seeking input from students, colleagues, and even parents to assess the effectiveness of teaching methods and classroom management strategies. By viewing feedback as a valuable opportunity for growth rather than criticism, educators can make informed adjustments to their practices. For example, a teacher might implement anonymous surveys to gather students' thoughts on lesson effectiveness, allowing them to refine their approaches based on student preferences and needs. This openness not only enhances teaching practices but also models a growth mindset for students, encouraging them to embrace constructive criticism in their own learning.

Embrace Change

In the dynamic field of education, change is inevitable— whether it's new curricular standards, technological advancements, or shifts in student demographics. Teachers who embrace change exhibit adaptability by being willing to revise their approaches and explore new methodologies. This might involve professional development workshops, collaborating with peers to share best practices, or integrating innovative technologies into their lessons. For instance, a teacher might transition to a blended learning model, combining traditional teaching with online resources to enhance student engagement and accommodate different learning styles. By demonstrating a positive attitude toward change, educators inspire their students to be flexible and resilient in the face of challenges.

Experiment with New Approaches

Experimentation is a key component of adaptability, as it allows teachers to explore new teaching methods and assess their effectiveness in real-time. This could involve trying out project-based learning, inquiry-based approaches, or incorporating multimedia resources into lessons. By piloting new strategies, teachers can identify what works best for their students and refine their practices accordingly. For instance, a teacher might implement a flipped classroom model, where students review content at home and engage in hands-on activities in class, promoting active learning and collaboration. This willingness to experiment fosters a culture of innovation in the classroom, encouraging students to take risks in their own learning and develop critical thinking skills.

2. Spiritual Development

Integrate Ethical Discussions

Engaging students in discussions about ethics and morality helps them understand the importance of values in their lives. This practice not only fosters critical thinking but also encourages students to explore their beliefs and develop a moral compass. By addressing ethical dilemmas related to various subjects, teachers can promote a deeper understanding of right and wrong and the implications of their actions.

Good Support System (Caring, Nurturing)

Establishing a caring and nurturing classroom environment is crucial for students' spiritual development. When teachers provide emotional support and create safe spaces for students to express themselves, they foster trust and openness. This supportive atmosphere allows students to thrive academically and personally, encouraging them to explore their identities and beliefs without fear of judgment.

Integrate Real-World Applications

Connecting classroom lessons to real-world situations enhances students' understanding of how their learning impacts their lives and the world around them. By integrating real-world applications, teachers can demonstrate the relevance of academic content and encourage students to think critically about their roles in society. This practice helps students recognize the interconnectedness of knowledge, values, and their potential contributions to the community.

Reflect on Your Own Practice

Teachers should regularly engage in self-reflection to assess their teaching practices and personal growth. By evaluating their experiences and seeking areas for improvement, educators can better understand how their spiritual beliefs influence their teaching. This reflective practice not only enhances their effectiveness but also models the importance of self-awareness and lifelong learning for their students.

Strategies to Encourage Lifelong Learning in Students

1. Encourage Curiosity and Questioning

Create an environment where students feel comfortable asking questions and exploring topics that interest them. By valuing their inquiries, educators can stimulate a sense of wonder and a desire to seek knowledge beyond the classroom.

2. Inquiry-Based Learning

Implement inquiry-based learning approaches that allow students to investigate and research topics actively. This method fosters critical thinking and encourages students to take ownership of their learning through exploration and discovery.

3. Independent Projects Related to Interests

Encourage students to pursue independent projects that align with their passions and interests. This autonomy fosters engagement and allows students to delve deeper into subjects they are passionate about, cultivating a lifelong love for learning.

4. Critical Thinking Skills

Teach critical thinking skills by challenging students to analyze information, evaluate sources, and make informed decisions. This skill set empowers students to approach problems thoughtfully and enhances their ability to learn independently.

5. Groups Where Students Share Ideas

Organize collaborative groups that encourage students to share ideas, work on solutions, and learn from one another. This peer interaction promotes a sense of community and enables students to benefit from diverse perspectives.

6. Personalized Learning

Tailor learning experiences to meet the unique needs and interests of each student. By offering differentiated instruction, educators can ensure that students remain engaged and motivated to learn at their own pace.

7. Model Lifelong Learning

Demonstrate a commitment to lifelong learning by sharing personal experiences of growth and development. When teachers model this mindset, students are more likely to adopt similar attitudes toward their own education.

8. Technology Integration

Utilize technology to enhance learning experiences and provide access to a wealth of resources. Incorporating digital tools encourages students to explore new information and engage with content in innovative ways.

9. Growth Mindset

Foster a growth mindset by emphasizing the value of effort and persistence. Encouraging students to embrace challenges and view failures as opportunities for growth instills resilience and a lifelong commitment to learning.

10. Connect Learning to Real-World Applications

Help students understand the relevance of their studies by connecting lessons to real-world scenarios. This approach enhances motivation and demonstrates how knowledge can be applied in practical situations, encouraging ongoing exploration and learning.

The Teacher's Role in Shaping the Future of Students and Education

1. Instilling a Love of Learning

By fostering a positive and engaging learning environment, teachers can inspire students to develop a genuine curiosity and passion for knowledge. This love of learning encourages students to pursue education beyond the classroom, leading to lifelong growth.

2. Encouraging Critical Analysis and Thoughtful Questions

Teachers can guide students in analyzing information and considering diverse perspectives, equipping them with the skills to navigate complex situations. By promoting inquiry and critical thinking, educators prepare students to make informed decisions in their personal and professional lives.

3. Building Social/Emotional Intelligence

By integrating social-emotional learning into their curriculum, teachers help students develop empathy, resilience, and effective communication skills. These attributes are crucial for personal success and contribute to a positive classroom environment and society.

4. Promoting Equity and Inclusion

Teachers play a vital role in creating inclusive classrooms where all students feel valued and respected. By embracing diversity and promoting equity, educators help students understand and appreciate different backgrounds, fostering a sense of community.

5. Adapting to Changing Needs

In a rapidly evolving educational landscape, teachers must be flexible and responsive to the changing needs of their students. This adaptability ensures that instruction remains relevant and effective, addressing individual learning styles and challenges.

6. Advocating for Student Needs

Educators can serve as advocates for their students, ensuring that their voices are heard and their needs are met. By championing for resources and support, teachers can help create a more conducive learning environment.

7. Modeling Positive Behaviors

Teachers serve as role models, demonstrating positive behaviors such as respect, kindness, and perseverance. By modeling these traits, educators influence students to adopt similar behaviors in their interactions with peers and in their future endeavors.

8. Encouraging Creativity and Innovation

By fostering an environment that values creativity and innovation, teachers can inspire students to think outside the box and approach problems from different angles. This encouragement nurtures the next generation of thinkers and problem solvers.

9. Preparing Students for the World of Work and Tomorrow's Challenges

Educators can equip students with essential skills for the workforce, such as collaboration, communication, and adaptability. By focusing on real-world applications and challenges, teachers prepare students to thrive in an ever-changing job market.

Ensuring Continued Growth and Impact on Students' Lives

1. Identify Student Strengths and Build on Them

Recognizing and nurturing each student's unique strengths fosters confidence and motivation. By tailoring instruction to leverage these strengths, educators can enhance student engagement and promote a growth mindset.

2. Demonstrate Unwavering Support

Conveying to students that you are there for them, genuinely care, and will not give up fosters a trusting relationship. This support encourages students to take risks in their learning and seek help when needed, knowing they have a reliable advocate.

3. Acknowledge the Impact of Culture

Understanding the diverse cultural backgrounds of students allows educators to create a more inclusive learning environment. By incorporating culturally relevant materials and perspectives, teachers can better connect with students and validate their experiences.

4. Focus on Each Student's Unique Contributions

Emphasizing that all students have the ability to learn and contribute encourages a sense of belonging. By celebrating diversity and individual contributions, educators cultivate a positive classroom culture that values every student's input.

5. Assess Growth in Every Learning Experience

Regularly assessing student growth, not just in grades but in overall development, provides insights into their progress. This holistic approach allows educators to adjust their teaching methods and recognize achievements that might otherwise go unnoticed.

6. Continuously Examine Your Practice

Engaging in self-reflection and professional development is essential for growth as an educator. By examining teaching practices and seeking feedback, teachers can identify areas for improvement and adapt to better meet the needs of their students.

Actions to Create a Lasting Impact on Students and the Community

1. Implement Team-Building Activities

Regularly incorporating team-building activities fosters collaboration and trust among students. These activities help students develop essential social skills and create a supportive classroom environment that encourages positive relationships.

2. Foster an Inclusive Classroom

Striving to create an inclusive environment ensures that all students feel welcome and valued. This holistic approach recognizes the diverse needs of each student, promoting a sense of belonging and enhancing their overall learning experience.

3. Encourage Open Communication

Establishing open lines of communication invites students to share their thoughts and concerns. This transparency creates a safe space for dialogue, enabling students to feel heard and respected, which is vital for their emotional and academic growth.

4. Cultivate Empathy and Respect

Actively promoting empathy and respect among students encourages a supportive classroom culture. By modeling these values, teachers help students develop strong interpersonal skills and a deeper understanding of their peers' perspectives.

5. Support School and Out-of-School Activities

Engaging in both school and extracurricular activities strengthens the connection between students, families, and the community. This involvement not only enriches students' educational experiences but also fosters a sense of pride and investment in their school.

6. Keep Stakeholders Informed

Maintaining regular communication with stakeholders, including parents and community members, builds a collaborative support system. Keeping them informed about student progress and classroom initiatives enhances community engagement and support for educational goals.

7. Hold Students Accountable

Encouraging personal accountability helps students understand the importance of their actions and decisions. By setting clear expectations and consequences, educators empower students to take responsibility for their learning and behavior.

8. Model Positive Behavior

Demonstrating how a good person should act provides students with a real-life example of positive behavior. By embodying values such as kindness, integrity, and perseverance, educators inspire students to adopt similar traits in their own lives.

Conclusion

In conclusion, teaching is more than just a job—it's a calling. It's about making a difference, one student at a time, by creating a classroom environment where students feel valued, supported, and inspired to reach their full potential. Throughout this book, we've explored practical strategies to help you become the best educator you can be—whether it's through building strong relationships, staying adaptable, or fostering a positive, inclusive learning environment.

As you reflect on the lessons shared here, remember that teaching is a journey of continuous growth. It's about understanding your students, meeting them where they are, and helping them take the next steps in their learning. But it's also about understanding yourself—your strengths, your areas for growth, and the impact you can have on those around you. Every small change you make, whether it's adjusting your teaching style, offering a listening ear, or taking the time to learn from your colleagues, adds up to something bigger.

Don't forget that being an educator means being a lifelong learner. Stay open to new ideas, be willing to adapt when things don't go as planned, and embrace the challenges along the way. Your impact goes far beyond what you teach in the classroom; it extends to the way you shape the hearts and minds of your students, inspiring them to become lifelong learners, critical thinkers, and empathetic individuals who can contribute positively to the world.

Ultimately, the most powerful tool you have as an educator is your ability to connect with your students and with others in your school community. When you lead with empathy, understanding, and a willingness to grow, you create an environment where everyone can succeed—together.

As you move forward, continue to reflect, adapt, and push yourself to be the teacher you know you can be. The work you do matters more than you can imagine. Keep making a difference, and know that your efforts are shaping the future, one student at a time.